MY SOUL'S 200
JOURNEYS

Firsthand Detailed Accounts on True Events

MY SOUL'S
200
JOURNEYS

HENRY C WONG

To my Teacher, in my past, present and future,
I am forever grateful.

"Na Mor Bun Schi Da Zi Zai Wan Fo"

May the 9words Mantra accompany
ALL in my journeys.

CONTENTS

Introduction. **13**

Journeys **17**

001-051809   Out of Body Experience 18

002-051909   Vibrational Shock 19

003-052309   A Wild Ride. 20

004-060309 My Ultimate Safeguard 22

005-061609   Pounding from the Vibrations. 23

006-062109   Mystery of the Totems 24

007-062209   Over my Body 25

008-063009 Message for Reflection 26

009-071109   Consciousness Based Realities 27

010-071309   Animal Realm. 28

011-091409   Deep Hidden Emotion 30

012-092109   True Reflection 32

013-092409   Unfading Love   33

014-012610   Everything Spins. 34

015-012710   Knowing before Showing 35

016-051010   Out of Routine 36

017-051210   Realistic Sensation 37

018-051310   Plasma Sphere. 38

019-060910   An Unusual Routine 40

020-061110   Many Versions of Me 41

021-080910   Traveling in a Spaceship 43

022-081610   Different Anatomy 45

023-082610   Guardian Dark Angels 46

024-092910   The Invisible Acrobat 48

025-093010   Exploration in Space. 49

026-100110   Who's in the Mirror 50

027-100710   Seamless Passage 51

028-102210   Realities are Chosen. 53

029-110110   Shadowy Arms 55

030-110510 Slideshow 57
031-112010 Guanyin Temple 59
032-121910 Image of Time 61
033-010811 My Childhood Friend 63
034-011111 My Previous Life 65
035-012911 Looking for 3 Suns 67
036-013011 Purple Spaceship 69
037-020111 Images from Beyond 70
038-020711 Incoherent Scenes 71
039-021411 Take me to the Moon 72
040-021911 Flying with a Girl 73
041-041811 My Dear two Sons. 75
042-061511 Who's Flying 76
043-061611 Going Through the Wall. 77
044-062011 Blessing Los Angeles 78
045-070111 Himalayas Top. 79
046-070311 Left Eye Seeing .81
047-071411 Majestic Scenery 82
048-071611 Universality of Empathy 84
049-072411 Blind Faith in Myself 86
050-072911 A Beautiful Train Ride. 88
051-073011 Dancing to the Beat of the Universe 90
052-080811 Crashing through the Atrium 92
053-080911 A Message from my Sons 94
054-081411 Seeing without Knowing 96
055-081511 Number 11. 98
056-081611 Stretching the Imagination 100
057-081911 The Face Shifter 102
058-082611 Blessings for All. 104
059-082911 Social Gatherings 106
060-090211 Year 1556 108
061-091411 A Science Field Trip 110
062-092611 Southern California. 112
063-100711 Body Soul Misalignment 114
064-102511 Authentic Requests 116

065-111111 Go with the Flow 118
066-121711 Promise Kept 120
067-123011 Visiting my Neighbor 122
068-010712 Mirror Mirror. 123
069-012612 Intermixing of Images. 124
070-013012 Superimposed Body. 125
071-021312 Sleep Paralysis 126
072-022312 Secret Message. 127
073-022512 I must be Dreaming 129
074-022712 Women in Pictures 130
075-030512 Nonphysical Reality 132
076-030912 The Nonphysical Pain. 134
077-031512 Who's Watching 135
078-040512 Time vs Instant 136
079-041512 My Teacher. 137
080-042012 High Frequency Blue 139
081-042312 Living on Moon 140
082 042412 Hovering Machine. 142
083-050412 Free Spirit 143
084-050512 Transduction of Thoughts .145
085-051612 Borders between Realms .146
086-060212 Realm of Transformations .148
087-060312 Girls' Voices 149
088-060412 Eternal Seeing. 151
089-060712 Follow the Dragon 152
090-060912 Kaleidoscopic Experience. 154
091-061212 It Happened Twice 156
092-061312 Marvelous Explorations 158
093-061512 Meeting My Other Family .160
094-061812 Strange Realms 162
095-062112 Elusiveness of Time 164
096-062312 Repentance Prayer. 165
097-070712 One and Only Reality. 167
098-071812 The Big Bang. 169
099-072512 Sensation vs Image 170

100-081512 Love and Attachment 172

101-082412 Number 3245.................................173

102-082712 A Day at the Beach.........................175

103-082812 My Seashore House 176

104-083012 Telekinesis 177

105-083112 The Ever-Changing Universe 178

106-091212 Spectacular Wonders.......................179

107-091512 Party Crasher.............................. 181

108-092912 Buddha in Chinese Character 183

109-100212 Third Person Perspective 185

110-100412 A Familiar Stranger.........................187

111-100812 Nothing isn't Alive.........................188

112-101812 Instant Arrivals.............................190

113-102212 Positive Thoughts 191

114-102312 Images of Reality..........................192

115-102712 Spin like an Atom 194

116-102812 Busy Traveling 196

117-103012 Free Fall 198

118-110312 Change Scene.............................. 200

119-111712 Spiral Totem..............................201

120-112112 Mud Creatures............................ 203

121-112412 Self Perspectives 204

122-112512 A Touch of Reality 206

123-112612 Slow Detachments 207

124-113012 Similar but Different 208

125-120112 Alien Spaceship 210

126-120412 Busy Traveling............................212

127-120512 Disjointed Events 214

128-120612 People Everywhere 215

129-120712 Happy Flying 217

130-121212 Who Am I 218

131-121912 Sticky Filaments 220

132-122812 Sit up and Leave 221

133-122912 Fly Like an Eagle 222

134-010513 My Body's Missing 223

135-012513 Can Happen Anytime. 224
136-021213 Center of the Earth 225
137-021313 Kindness to All. 227
138-021513 Fatherly Love 228
139-021913 Family Reunion 229
140-022013 Roast Duck. 230
141-022113 A Mundane Session 232
142-030913 Da Zi Zai Wan Fo. 233
143-032313 Brighter Frequency. 235
144-032513 Dancing to the Music 236
145-033113 Push-up Within 238
146-040113 Families Everywhere 239
147-053113 Tibetan Connection 241
148-060813 My Soul Mate. 243
149-060913 Sensation of Zero Gravity 244
150-062213 A Night Out 246
151-071313 Fractal Totems. 247
152-072513 Remembrance of the Past. 249
153-072813 The Milky Way 250
154-080213 Reality Check. 252
155-080413 Tunnel Vision 253
156-080813 Buddhist Symbol 255
157-081213 Inner White Light. 256
158-081813 Upside Down. 258
159-082213 Faces of the Infinity 259
160-090213 Connected but Independent 260
161-091313 Breathing in the Nonphysical 261
162-091413 Where's my Altar. 262
163-091913 A Precious Experience. 263
164-092113 A Rainy Night. 264
165-100113 Detachment of Bodies 266
166-100813 Meeting my Teacher's Teacher 267
167-101413 A.D. and B.C. 269
168-101513 Parallel Realities 271

169-102713 Insensate Pinching 272

170-102913 Our Daughter Somewhere 274

171-110313 My Guardians. 275

172-111713 White Bright Light 276

173-120113 Music of the Mantra 277

174-121713 Human Anatomy 279

175-012714 Entities in Other Dimensions. 280

176-012814 Hanging Upside Down. .281

177-021014 Perception is Reality. 283

178-021514 Telephoto Vision 285

179-030414 My Other Wife 287

180-032814 A Terrifying Experience 289

181-092914 My Guiding Light. 291

182-100214 The Ultimate Void 292

183-102714 Buddha on the Wall 293

184-111014 Holding my Own Head. 294

185-121514 The Dormant Sentiment. 295

186-010515 Tahiti Revisited 297

187-042815 Empathy of the Essence 298

188-020316 Seamless Shifting of Realities. 299

189-021516 A Matter of Visualization 301

190-021916 Breathing under Water. 302

191-071816 The Voice to Remember 303

192-072516 My Threefold Perspectives 304

193-081116 We're the Worlds. 306

194-071918 Realities of Visualization 307

195-072418 My Inner Temple 308

196-081118 Portal in my Mind 309

197-082718 Deep into the Maze 310

198-030423 Leaping between Realms 312

199-060823 Infinite Double Doors 314

200-071523 Watching and Feeling 315

Conclusion. **317**

INTRODUCTION

During the idling days at home in the year of 2020, I couldn't avoid the calling for self-reflection at my retirement age. After over 40 years of being a healthcare provider in Los Angeles, finally, I had a chance to think about "the meaning of life," types of questions. As a Buddhist since the year of 2000, I have often pondered over what I can share with the world in this lifetime.

One day, I was reading over the journals that I had kept for all my out-of-body events. A lot of them were being read for the first time since I had recorded them. To my surprise, there had been over 200 times of out-of-body occurrences from the year of 2009 to 2018, mostly in the first 5 years.

After reading through all of them, I noticed that all 200 events were different. Surprisingly, every event had a unique story to tell, and they were both unpredictable and unfathomable. Nevertheless, the details in the course of the events could give us a glimpse of the inner workings of the soul and other realms.

The book's ultimate goal is to demonstrate convincingly the existence of one's soul. By putting yourself in my place through these journeys, you might indirectly get to realize your own soul. Once the inner connection is triggered, it will guide you in making decisions among seemingly difficult choices in the physical world. With the overwhelming amount of spiritually related information available, this book can also serve as a point of reference to evaluate and further develop your personal spirituality.

The book won't necessarily bring you the answers that you are currently looking for. However, it could bring insights and faith with respect to one's true existential nature. Moreover, a great number of details in the 200 out-of-body events, can also bring clarity and different perspectives from beyond to our mundane lives.

The phenomenon of a soul entity leaving the physical body is fundamentally existential. The book has sufficient accounts to reasonably support the existence of soul among all of us in this universe. When it does happen, it would leave an indelible memory deep in our psyche.

Meditation was an important part in preparing all my journeys. It forces me to remain in a static physical position, which can exhaust my body's natural, restless tendency. All the while, my mind becomes fatigue and thoughts diminish, devoid of any desire and vexation. This is one way of clearing my mind. At this "meditative" state, my soul would come through with manifestations from my nonphysical dimension.

However, there's no telling as to what and when it can happen. For my soul to emerge on its own volition, one important condition is to surrender my control, down to its most subtle level. And this is one difficult and moreover, a scary thing to do. This book is not meant to encourage readers to embark on such an endeavor, due to its unpredictability.

"Na Mor Bun Schi Da Zi Zai Wan Fo" was the 9words Mantra that I recited in many of the events. It had proven to me time and time again that it elevated the positivity of many downright scary scenes. It also manifested some amazing events in some of those journeys. The Mantra was the only thing from the physical world that would accompany me in the nonphysical realm. It has blessed me with the courage and faith that I badly needed at times.

One potential problem which I expected would be the strong opinions towards this sensitive subject. However, that encouraged me to come up with ways to transcend a myriad of possible divides. The journeys were recorded immediately afterwards, in simplistic and fundamental wording. Furthermore, the book tried to exclude names for privacy reason, except those in the public domain. It also avoided using any external terminology and interpretations, reference and citation, to maintain its objectivity. After all, the main goal is to share the out-of-body events as it happened in an uncharted territory.

There are designated numbers for each event before the title. The first 3-digit serial number of each event is in a chronological order. The last 6-digit number is the date of the event, in month-day-year format. The titles and italicized phrases were my subjective insights in retrospect. The original records of the events were handwritten in English on a hardbound journal on the same day of each event. Often, they were recorded right after I woke up from the event. To keep it true and authentic, I avoided any outside paraphrasing or editing alteration, to preserve the "original feel" towards the scenes of the events.

You might find something from these 200 events that would resonate with "You", or newfound perception of the world. Despite the apparent duality between the mundane and spiritual, they are inseparable as one existence from which we all can gather our experiences.

JOURNEYS

001-051809
OUT OF BODY EXPERIENCE

You just never know until ...

Today marked 43 consecutive days of two hours meditation. Afterwards, it was still early before dawn. I was tired and went back to bed. Suddenly, vibrations similar to electrical shock came on throughout my entire body. During this half-asleep transition state, I was aware of my thoughts and feelings.

Soon after, I saw all the buildings collapsing around me. At that moment, I spotted a patch of blue sky up above. I just had this feeling that I flew at other places before. Then I took off flying straight up so fast that the earth behind me disappeared in a flash.

It was misty and I was just floating in space. I was also holding an unrecognizable large insect which was encased in a clear bubble. There were also a lot of other sparkling spheres floating around. This was my first out of body experience.

002-051909
VIBRATIONAL SHOCK

It happened back-to-back, two days in a row.

Today, I wanted to repeat what had happened yesterday. After my usual two hours meditation, I went back to bed. Vibrations akin to electrical current again ran through my body from head to toe. It began with short bursts of zapping and gradually increased in duration, intensity and areas of the body.

It was the last long one that led me to roll to the right and floating off the bed. It seemed like some force carrying me off. I was also floating upright in my bedroom.

My consciousness was merely observing without questions. Thoughts were direct knowing but not reasoning. I also easily drifted out of that state to check my clock. The entire experience lasted for about 20 minutes.

003-052309

A WILD RIDE

It's no longer just a fluke.

After the morning meditation, I went back to bed. I was not conscious of when I fell asleep. I was awakened by a loud screeching sound. I found myself driving a car towards an intersection, struggling to slow down and turning left without rolling over. I couldn't recall anyone anywhere. Then I was traveling down a road which turned into a tunnel with sand blowing across the road. The tunnel began rotating, twisting and turning until I couldn't keep the car on the road. In an instant, I floated off the road and it got calm and quiet. I was just floating through space.

This time, I didn't have any feeling of my body. It felt like just my consciousness floating. There were patterns of colors and lights that kept changing around me.

At one moment, I started to think about people and beings. At once, a large image of just the eyes and top half of the face appeared. I warned myself not to think randomly but to maintain a state of no thoughts. Nevertheless, all the appearances were colorful, soothing and peaceful.

Suddenly, everything disappeared. I found myself with a body showing up in a household in India. There was a man with his daughter talking to me. I was wondering at the time if I had reincarnated in India. I was also curious if I would be able to go back to where I was from. As soon as I had that thought of worry, I gradually drifted back into my physical body. All these happened in about 7 minutes since I lay in bed.

004-060309
MY ULTIMATE SAFEGUARD

My only way to fight fear was the 9wordsMantra.

After meditation, I went back to bed. While I was lying on my right side, vibrations started. From mild to strong, it was the fourth time that triggered the out of body movements. Before I sat up and rolled to the side, I started to recite the 9words Mantra as my safeguard.

The only thing that I could see were streams of black filaments rushing by me. At times, they paused but continuously passed by me. There were also constant inhuman sounds by my sides. However, I did hear few times of apparent human sounds.

I remembered to tell myself not to be afraid, just take a plunge and go where it would take me. Abruptly, it all just stopped, and my physical eyes opened seamlessly. The entire experience took about 15 minutes. The 9words Mantra didn't change the images but without it, I probably wouldn't have enough courage to continue till the end.

005-061609

POUNDING FROM THE VIBRATIONS

My past lives began manifesting.

After meditation, I went back to bed. At first, I had this subtle feeling followed by mild vibrations. And the strong ones were not far behind. This time, I was hearing loud clunking noise and feeling vibrations pounding all over my body. I felt the most pressure at my left kidney area. That just went on for quite a while.

Then I felt being carried off my bed. I reminded myself to keep calm, cool and just watch. Even if some scary images might show up. Soon after, I started to see black lines mixed with black dots rushing directly towards me and continuing to my peripheral. So, I started reciting the 9words Mantra.

Then I showed up at a place with a woman and two kids. I vividly remembered her face as if I had known her already. She was also looking back at me. But I couldn't recognize her.

I wanted to wake up and come back to the physical world. Shortly after, I woke up in a false awakening phase with my wife hugging me and asking me if I had to go to work. I thought I had already wakened up but not until I woke up without my wife being around. It all took about 20 minutes.

006-062109
MYSTERY OF THE TOTEMS

The universal language of the existence is totem.

After meditation, I went back to bed lying on my right side. With the vibrations, I floated away. This time, I saw a lot of totems like diagrams around me. They came in groups and clusters, but not rushing by me.

007-062209
OVER MY BODY

Of all things, my soul remembered to practice Mantra and Mudra.

As usual, I went back to bed after two hours of meditation. I was very tired, lying on my left side. When the strong vibrations came, I started reciting the 9words Mantra. I remembered thinking, if this experience was not proper, then the Mantra would make it disappear.

The recitation continued seamlessly well after the completion of my out of body movements. I found out reciting in the other realm was much more natural and effortless. One thing that stood out was that I made the Dharma Seal "Mudra" on both of my hands. I extended them out to the open and said loudly, "One Dharma Seal."

In this session, I hovered closely right over where my physical body was. I was rotating and turning without touching my body. I even felt clearly my face pressing against the headboard of my bed. I woke up thereafter. The session was 30' long.

008-063009
MESSAGE FOR REFLECTION

My soul saw only what was meant to be seen.

After meditation, I went back to bed. This time I felt more comfortable lying on my back. It happened in a flash, and I was floating all over the place in the room. There was also rhythmic music playing as I was flying around.

On a large transparent wall, I remembered seeing vividly and clearly 4 Chinese characters. The 4th character is so rare that I have never seen it before. It means tranquil and peaceful after some later research. The first 3 characters mean "my heart". There were many other words, but they were blurry and not readable. I was just so happy receiving such a meaningful and profound message.

Then I flew with such a joy to an ancient village and landed there. As I was waking up to a false awakening, I found my wife still at home and I wondered why she didn't go to work. It clocked at 7:10. Moment after, I woke up again just to realize she was already at work. And surprisingly, the clock also showed 7:10 when I opened my eyes. The whole session lasted for 15 minutes.

009-071109
CONSCIOUSNESS BASED REALITIES

My soul deems only the immediate incarnation as reality.

After 100' of meditation, I went back to bed and my wife was also in bed sleeping. As I was floating away, I realized that I was not breathing during the initial phase of separation from the body.

The sensation of having a body floating was limited mostly to the room. Once I took off flying straight up, I was able to speed up the flying. But I was not sure where to fly to.

I remembered calling for my Teacher followed by reciting the 9words Mantra. Again, the same random black filaments were flying towards me and off to my peripheral as described in the earlier session 004-060309.

I arrived at a place where people were doing exercise in a huge machine. When I felt that I was coming back, I drifted into a false awakening phase. Nevertheless, I was so sure that this must be where I was coming from. I woke up there at 7:25. I was playing with my nephew and my younger son. I started shouting to my older son and my wife to come in. I told them that I was from the future 2007. Moment later, when I finally woke up in the physical reality, the time was only 7:10.

010-071309
ANIMAL REALM

Animals are also part of the afterlife...

After 120' of meditation, I went back to bed. I was lying on my left side. I was trying not to compress my lungs and restricting my breathing. Once I was at ease, the phase of leaving the body took place. I was floating all over the room. Soon after, I blasted off flying into space from the top right part of the room.

I saw a figure looking like a horse. It seemed like I was flying through an animal realm. I said that to myself. They came in herds, but I could see only their silhouettes. I couldn't make out of what types they were. I told myself to concentrate on what I saw.

Next, I found myself landing in a place where there were people gathering. One person spotted me as an outsider. In a room, another person accused me of sabotaging something. Then I went out to the open and flew straight up to the sky.

After flying for a while, I landed at another place. At that moment, I was wondering what it would be like back in L.A., knowing clearly that's where I came from. I pulled out my cellphone and flipped it open. I saw symbols and formats that I didn't understand. I knew I was about to come back since everything was dissipating and fading out. I woke up this time without any false awakenings. It was a 15-minute-long session.

011-091409
DEEP HIDDEN EMOTION

The extent of emotions is stored deeply in my soul.

After 60' of meditation, I went back to bed at 7:25. Even though I had to be at work at 8:00. It didn't take long before I rolled off to the left edge of the bed. I stood erect right away In the room.

Those familiar black lines appeared again. I was pleased and excited to see them and I started reciting the 9words Mantra.The black lines totems were everywhere and continuously moving, changing, grouping, regrouping, forming lines and circles. They were scattered but also in formation. I was reciting the 9words Mantra the whole time. Unfortunately, I couldn't understand their hidden meanings at all.

All of a sudden, I had this thought of flying out but nothing happened. I said to myself that all these were not for me to control. Thereafter, I showed up in a cold and snowy place like the base of a ski lift with a lot of young people around. I remembered talking to my son and then I walked away.

Next, I thought I woke up and looked at the clock showing 11:44. I said to myself that I was already late to work at 8:00. The clock was not a digital one that I had in my physical reality.

Later I saw eye examination machines on both sides of my bed. I called out for my wife. She came in with bandages on her eyes, telling me she had eye surgery. Then my daughter and son were preparing something for my eyes. I sternly declined. I was wondering where I was. I asked for a calendar to find out the year. But they always became blurry as I got close to it.

The place started to look like an apartment in the old days. As I walked out to the front door, I saw my younger son in the kitchen. I called out his name and he came over. We hugged. He looked about 10 years of age, and I didn't recognize him. At that moment, I just broke down and cried my heart out. Slowly I woke up with tears still in my eyes. My digital clock was showing 7:44. All these happened in about only 20 minutes. Quickly I rushed off to work 10 minutes late.

012-092109
TRUE REFLECTION

How my soul would perceive itself...

After meditation in my study, I went back to bed in my bedroom. Nothing happened until I was totally relaxed without a bit of anxious feeling. I was lying on my left but felt the rolling to the right off the bed. I was stuck very closed to the floor around the bed. I felt restricted and attempted to command myself to fly off but to no avail.

Moment later, I showed up in a room like my bathroom. I heard loud noises which didn't mean anything. I was swiping the white cabinet below the counter with both hands side to side but couldn't see my hands on the cabinet. When I looked up to the large wall mirror, I couldn't see myself very clearly in the mirror. Back into the bedroom, I saw people hauling something. Soon after, I woke up. Session was 15 minutes long.

013-092409
UNFADING LOVE

My soul carries the energy of emotion that we call love.

After meditation, I went back to bed lying on my left side. I was out unconscious for a while until I became aware that nothing was happening. Right at that moment, I felt something was about to come. I kept myself still and waited. The vibrations came continuously in short and fast bursts until the final big one.

During this time, I heard radio music quite loud. I felt the violent shaking through the whole room and my bed. My body and blanket were shaking hard while I was floating off to the left corner. From there to the right corner of the room where I stood up.

Immediately after, I started to fly away. I noticed that the speed was slow. I showed up in a room like my real bedroom. I saw a cute and pleasant baby about a year old sitting up in bed. He looked like my younger son. I was holding both of his hands and looked straight into his eyes and face. He kept saying something like "Ju Bah Jah ..." to me. That lasted for a while until I was moved by him. I started weeping with joy and slowly woke up with no false awakening, ending a session of 28 minutes.

014-012610
EVERYTHING SPINS

My soul could rotate and revolve...

It had been almost four months since I had my last cross-over. After 2 hours of meditation, I went back to bed. Neighbor's dogs were barking. I was not aware of when I drifted into unconsciousness.

Only after I became awakened, I started experiencing the vibrations multiple times. That in turn led to me floating out of the body. This was the first time that both of my legs lifted high up. Subsequently, I was also floating upright and spinning around my own axis.

I remembered that I said, "Ready to fly", but I didn't go very far. I called on my sister and parents to show them how I spun around. I was so certain that I belonged to that seemingly real existence until I woke up.

015-012710
KNOWING BEFORE SHOWING

My soul seemed to know the scripts in advance.

After 2 hours of meditation, I went back to sleep at 5:00. This time, it was quick without much of any vibrations. I was rolling off the bed with my feet spearheading towards the bedroom door and quickly shooting to the left corner of the room.

There was something worth mentioning. Before I got to that final spot, I knew already in advance that I would go from horizontal to vertical. I certainly did and I was hovering above, looking down at the bed. I saw my wife on her side of the bed. I also saw myself in bed where I usually slept. This was the first time for me to see myself in bed.

I drifted quickly to where my wife's nightstand was. Again, I knew in advance that I was going to fly before I even got there, but I didn't experience much flying.

Shortly after, I became enormous in size. I was like a giant looking closely at some tiny model size spaceships with a peculiar design. I woke up thereafter. Session was 10 minutes total without any false awakening.

016-051010
OUT OF ROUTINE

_____

It can happen anytime...   _____

I went to bed around 11:45 last night. I didn't meditate beforehand. I felt the vibrations coming and simply just allowed it to play out. My legs felt very light, and they started floating up. I said to myself that legs must be light to fly. I was just floating all over the room, bumping the walls but not able to fly. I floated over my wife and landed on her side of the floor next to the bed. I screamed out loud wanting to get out of the dream because I couldn't fly away.

Apparently, my scream woke up my wife. She also screamed and rolled to the side of the bed. I went over to touch her hair and calm her down. I remembered her hair felt so real but knowing full well, this was not the physical reality. Nevertheless, I was just marveling at the sense of realism.

In one instant, I was simultaneously aware of sleeping on the left side of the bed and kneeling by the right side of the bed comforting my wife. I woke up at 12:12 am. This was the first time that would happen late in the night instead of the morning, and without prior meditation.

017-051210
REALISTIC SENSATION

How my soul could feel just as well...

After an hour of morning meditation, I went back to bed. I felt the vibrations and I knew the crossover was about to happen. Nothing much was happening until I noticed someone hovering over me while I was sleeping on my right side. That was exactly how I positioned myself in real time.

As I turned slightly to the left, I was unable to see the facial features of my wife. Nevertheless, I knew it was her. I remembered the realistic sensation when I was holding her hand. It felt exactly how I would feel holding her hand in the physical reality. She then started making a lot of noise by shaking her leg. Gradually, I woke up and saw myself still sleeping on my right side.

018-051310
PLASMA SPHERE

My soul went through a lot in a short time...

After 60' of meditation, I went back to bed. I drifted into unconsciousness for an unknown amount of time before becoming awakened. I started for the first time to concentrate on the images in my mind. That in turn brought about the vibrations. The more I focused, the stronger were the vibrations. After a few times, I put in more effort and stayed focus longer. The shocks of the vibrations became much stronger, until I saw a large clear glass sphere filled with electrical sparks.

Right after that, it was like crossing over an imaginary interface to another realm and everything settled down. I was slightly concerned but I calmed down and surrendered to the movements. I started floating and flipping around. The floating didn't last too long, and I settled right next to my side of the bed.

I was staring at the blue flowers' patterns on the white bed sheet, similar to the blue design on Chinese porcelain vase. I was also saying to myself that I had exactly this same patterned bed sheet in my physical reality.

At that time, my wife and my older son showed up. He was in his current age of 20s. I asked them," When you saw me, was I leaning by the side of the bed or sleeping on my left side in bed?" They said that I was sitting on the floor and leaning next to the bed. I was wondering if I actually moved from the bed to the floor.

During that puzzling moment, I woke up to the physical reality. I didn't move from my original left side sleeping position at all. On top of that, I couldn't find a bed sheet with that same pattern of blue flowers on white. Nevertheless, it looked so familiar as if I had it before. The session was 20' long.

019-060910
AN UNUSUAL ROUTINE

Full body vibration prepared my soul to leave the body.

After drinking tea at 10:30 last night, I was especially alert. I was lying in bed on my left side, relaxed but not asleep until 1:30 am. Later I switched back to be flat on my back, but not worrying about not falling asleep. I had no thoughts of wanting to fall asleep but just passively waiting.

Slowly and gradually, vibrations came and took off. Right before that happened, I saw a lot of squares with yellowish gold color circle in the center. Once my body was totally submerged in the vibrations, I started floating upward. My feet first headed towards and over my wife who was sleeping on my right. Vividly, I felt my body erecting upright and revolving around a fixed axis. I also had this urge to recite the 9words Mantra. Then I heard faintly a knocking sound "da da" from a child, which didn't last long before I woke up.

020-061110
MANY VERSIONS OF ME

I am my soul, my body and their observer.

After 60' of meditation, I went back to bed lying on my left. I wasn't sure if I had drifted into dreams before I awakened. Nothing was happening until I sensed the mild vibrations. This time I noticed it in my head area. It was those intense vibrations that would ultimately complete the out of body phase.

At the same time, my wife was walking into the bedroom to her bathroom. I didn't really want to stop the process because of her interruption. I wanted to speed up the process. So, I was focusing more on the stronger vibration for faster crossing to the other side. Even before the crossover, I felt my wife coming over from behind and touched me. Of course, later in the day, she denied ever touching me. This meant that I was already not in the physical realm.

Once I floated up slightly, I knew that my mind shouldn't wander off or be thinking of something else. I would roll off to the left side. Immediately, I stood up and moved to the right of the room.

As I moved further along, I turned around and saw lots of apparent medical equipments in couple adjacent rooms. I also saw a nurse like person working. At that time, I tried to tell myself to fly away since I didn't like having my feet touching the floor, but to no avail. My feet ended up resting entirely on the floor.

I was moving around and being very curious about what was written on those small packages all over the room. I was able to zoom in but still too blurry to read. However, as I flipped through one bundle, I did recognize the Disney character "Porky Pig". As I was moving through few connecting closets, I was concerned being trapped in these tight spaces.

Since I knew I was capable of flying, I wanted to fly off a top floor in a tall building. There were two glass doors beginning to close in front of me, apparently keeping me from flying away. The building was situated high up on a cliff facing the ocean. Nevertheless, I somehow directed the doors to stay open and I flew away.

Suddenly, from another perspective, I was watching a very small version of myself flying. I also saw him, or myself rather, with a lot of other guys in an open space trying to fly. I presumed as an observer that I was also flying.

Moment later, I saw a person on my back pulling an arrow out of me. I screamed but without any feeling of pain. Right away, I woke up. It had been about 20 minutes. My mind was clear, and my body was at ease.

021-080910
TRAVELING IN A SPACESHIP

My soul somehow enjoyed space travel...

After 2 hours of meditation, I went back to bed lying on my usual left side. When I was able to hear my heartbeat, I switched to the right side due to the interference to my tranquil state. Vibrations were coming and going but not progressive. My wife's phone alarm went off in another room causing a short interruption. I maintained my composure and submitted myself to the crossover. At first, I rolled over and slid down to the left side. Then I was moving in a supine position with my head in front, circling around the bed. I kept reminding myself to be composed.

There was this continuous engine noise, "chun chun....". As I was approaching the right side of the room by the glass window, I felt my knee being pressed uncomfortably again the window. Shortly, I continued moving on to the area by the bathroom. There was no window but that was the place where I took off to somewhere else.

When I peeked through an opening, I saw the expanse of the universe and countless of stars. I was excited knowing that I was about to fly up to see the universe.

While I was traveling out to the universe, the same engine sound was heard. I did feel like being part of a slow-moving spaceship of some kind. I observed a string of colorful diamond shaped objects, going from moving in a straight line to forming a circle.

Gradually, everything just faded out. While I was traveling back to my room, I was looking through a small round window of a spaceship into the universe. I woke up afterwards. It was a 15-minute session.

022-081610
DIFFERENT ANATOMY

My soul doesn't seem like to have a life span.

After 2 hours of meditation, I went back to bed. I had a hard time to find a comfortable sleeping position. Finally, I settled in a position flat on my back with both arms crossed above my head, keeping the blanket up to block the sunlight. There was this very subtle and short burst of vibration acting as the telltale sign. The vibrations came and I crossed over, floating up in a supine position. I was going around the bed with my head in the front. I felt my feet dragging a little on the floor.

This was my first time that I experienced pressure in my bladder and groin area. Again, there was this continuous engine sound just as before while I was floating. When I looked straight across at my groin area, I saw the skeleton of my pelvis. There was a constant changing cluster of bright colors in the middle of the abdominal cavity, with the pelvic cage around.

As I moved towards the ceiling, I saw a spaceship like structure and a patch of open space. I wanted to go flying but my attempt didn't work out. Instead, everything was fading away and I slowly woke up.

023-082610
GUARDIAN DARK ANGELS

My soul knows its own past...

This time the vibrations came upon me before my regular sleep of the night. I was tired but very relaxed. I got that subtle signal and waited. It happened very fast. The vibrations didn't even last all that long as usual before I was off floating. I was moving headfirst in a supine position, with my upper half slightly lower than my lower half. I was going around and around very fast all over the room. I could feel the drapes at times with my feet.

Then the scene changed. My wife and a strange looking baby happened to be right next to me. I knew he was not my baby. My wife told me that he was someone else's baby. Then I just woke up. Before I even tried to recall everything that happened, another vibration came very fast and triggered a second crossover in the same night.

I ended up in some place where I could see clips of events and images of solitaire diamond. I remembered telling myself to memorize these images due to their potential significance. The tail of an airplane with the name partially revealed. Someone said Cuba. Men seemed like some kind of professionals next to a piece of equipment.

At that time, I felt my feet slipping and I wasn't able to stay still. This part got strange. I saw four short, dark and cloud like shadows carrying me and dropped me off in my bed. Then three of them rushed off and gone. The one remained was holding my left hand and it felt cold. I saw it was not like a human hand but some long curly structures. I got very emotional and broke down in tears. I said I was so happy.

I also saw 4 persons all wearing the same T-shirts before I started crying. They were talking to one person at the foot of my bed. I woke up with no tears in my eyes. All took about 40 minutes, but it felt like only few minutes with no detectable gaps throughout the whole experience. The atmosphere was joyous and not dark.

024-092910
THE INVISIBLE ACROBAT

━━━━━━━━━

My soul could be quite active...

After 2 hours of meditation, I went back to bed. Vibrations came and I was wondering if my erection would interfere with the crossover, apparently not. I remembered to recite the 9words Mantra during the crossover.

I was rolling to the sides, to my back, to the front, uprighting, rotating and spinning. I was so used to it by now that I could no longer remember all the fine details anymore.

However, I remembered reciting the 9words Mantra continuously throughout all the spinning. The 9words Mantra didn't stop the spinning and I was not aware of when it was over. At the time, I was quiet and submissive, since I came to realize that all those seemingly random scenes had their origins.

025-093010
EXPLORATION IN SPACE

My soul needed faith and courage into uncharted territory.

After 2 hours of meditation, I went back to bed. Before long, vibrations came and the out of body phase was completed. While I was moving around in the room, I remembered that I should be reciting the 9words Mantra to keep myself safe on the right path.

Furthermore, all these experiences were unknown to me. However, I just had faith that it would turn out the way it was supposed to. After a while, I stopped floating and went back lying in bed.

I couldn't recall when I drifted into another scene. I was flying in space and looking back, seeing a large rock formation traveling near me. The rock turned into a round object where we all landed in the middle of a very large pit.

There were sheer cliffs surrounding the pit. The wall of the cliffs looked melted and burned. There were houses and boats embedded in the walls. I was asking around on what year it was. I saw my wife and my kids, but they didn't give me the year. I was puzzled if it was the past or the future. I was also playing with a Doberman cub. Then I woke up when a goat tried to bite my face.

026-100110
WHO'S IN THE MIRROR

My soul knew who was in the mirror...

After 2 hours of meditation, I went back to bed, and I felt the signal. The noise my wife made around the room seemed to disrupt my hope to initiate any out of body movements. She left shortly after.

Surprisingly, I found myself turning into another visible and memorable person in the mirror. At the time, I could clearly remember his features. He was not good looking. He had a round face, small eyes and short tufts of mustache. When I told that to my mother, she became upset. So, I hugged and comforted her.

027-100710
SEAMLESS PASSAGE

_____

My soul is the portal to other realms.   _____

What a trip that I had this morning! After 2 hours of meditation, I felt quite alert going back to bed. During the out of body phase, I simply kept my mind still without actively doing anything. I wasn't thinking of surrendering, relaxation or breathing. The result was much better. Again, I rolled to the left until I left the body. I moved around a little bit around the room, stood up and approached a wall where I flew away.

I saw plenty of things on the ground that I did not recognize. They looked like toys. I landed in a crowd. A vehicle almost ran me over. I was making eye contacts with different people. It seemed like I knew them. Then I wanted to leave that place, and I flew away again.

I ended up against a wall and somehow, I just went through it into an apartment. I saw a woman whom I stared closely at her face. I couldn't recognize her or the couple children nearby, but I knew with certainty that they were my wife and kids.

Then suddenly, I had the urge to find out what year it was. I dug through a pile of paper, but they were in Korean. I asked her what year but whatever she said didn't make any sense to me. When I saw some pictures of Bruce Lee on the table, I broke down and cried. I came to realize that we existed in many worlds and time is irrelevant. She said a man should not cry like that.

I felt I was being out for a long time. I even remembered the story of someone wandering around in another realm for too long. Years went by in the physical reality even though it might seem like only a few minutes. I was a little worry and ran around wanting to go back.

Conversely, I was not thinking of "waking up" because I didn't have the notion of being out of my physical body and existing in another realm. In an instant, the scene faded out and the physical world faded in. Slowly I woke up. It all lasted about 25 minutes. This was the first time that I experienced consciously the crossover in reverse, from a nonphysical realm back into our physical reality, through a seamless direct passage.

028-102210
REALITIES ARE CHOSEN

---

*Realities are determined by the relevance
defined by my soul.*

After the morning meditation, I went back to bed. I couldn't remember drifting into a short dream state. At 7:38 am, I became aware and wanted to stay in just a little longer. I heard a sound apparently caused by my wife. So, I stayed still and waited for it to happen. Well, it happened so fast that vibrations weren't detected at all. I went straight into rolling, flipping, spinning and hovering. I could remember all those out of body movements. I got very closed to the floor without touching, right next to my bed.

Then I saw a bright yellow baseball sized object in front of me. I was floating throughout the the room following this thing which resembled an orchid. When we both reached the wall of the bathroom, I said to myself that we could go right through it. But we didn't and instead we turned around. It quickly disappeared and there was blue cloud appearing all around. During the whole time, there was always this repetitive knocking sound in the background.

Slowly I woke up to a sleeping position on my right side. I felt my wife snugged in bed from my left side. I also felt I was late to work. But at that same moment, I didn't believe that was my initial sleeping position which was on the left side. I was doubting how real was my wife next to me. Gradually, I woke up with my body lying on the left side. Time was only 7:45.

029-110110
SHADOWY ARMS

My soul was able to do mathematic calculations.

After meditation, I went back to bed at 7:15 am. I took up my sleeping position quickly on the left side. The scene shifting was quickly stabilized. I was floating all over the room in a supine position. After a while, I stood up and ended up at the bedroom door. I felt I was about to come out of this scene. Before that, I was looking forward to fly away somewhere else.

Unexpectedly I did something unusual. I was flapping my arms in front of myself. Surprisingly, I could see only undefined dark shadows of my arms and hands.

Next, I stood over my bed knowing that I could see my physical body. When I was lifting the bed sheet, there was somebody bouncing up and down. I saw a white kid seemed startled seeing me. And I was wondering if my appearance prompted his reaction.

I drifted into another scene where the clock was showing 7:50 am. The bed was gone. Instead, there were just rectangular pots with withered stalks in them. I did worry coming back too late and started getting panicky.

Without a pause, I found myself in another scene. A modest home I couldn't recognize. As I walked into the kitchen, my wife said to me, "You just got up." I asked her repeatedly, "What year is it?" I was trying to read the year off the paper on the wall. She said, "March 79." I uttered to myself, "I am from the future, 10 years later." I wanted to tell her and my two sons. I didn't get to see all their faces, but I just knew it's them. They couldn't hear me due to the loud noise. Soon after, I woke up and it was only 7:36 am.

030-110510
SLIDESHOW

The afterlife is not on a straight line...

Meditation for an hour before I went back to bed at 7:00 am. The crossover happened very fast, immediately followed by me floating around the room. At times, I would hit the closet doors. I was also aware of my body lying in bed and not wanting to go back into it. But when I got close to the bed, instantly, I got sucked back into the apparent physical body.

A moment after, there was the second crossover, and I got right back into the room once again. Looking out from my bedroom door, I saw all kinds of vivid colors before me. In the middle section of my view, I saw constantly changing images of apparent insects and prehistoric creatures. They appeared one after another as in a slideshow, except that being a 3D standalone hologram. I remembered my close friend warning me for not attaching to the enticing images in my experience.

To the right, it opened to a large room with simple furnishings, a small refrigerator, a recliner with an old man who lived there before I moved in. The walls and floors were old. I felt like I was going back in time to the house of the previous owner. I also saw a picture of him in the bathroom.

Apparently, I was back in time in my own home. Seemingly, I had traveled back to a time which I mistook as the real time of my physical reality. I saw cracked walls above my bed and nightstand. I said to my kids, "Oh no, this time travel had caused these damages." When I looked outside of the window, I saw broken walls and structures in other buildings. I was stunned and woke up at 7:18 am.

031-112010
GUANYIN TEMPLE

Strong preconceived beliefs persisted in my soul.

I woke up at 4:30 am to meditate for 2 hours. Afterwards, I went back to bed lying on my left side and kept everything still. Usually, I would just wait for it to happen. This time, I accidentally focused in the third eye area. This somehow triggered a very subtle and familiar telltale sign. So, I did it a few more times. Shortly after, I got out of my body and crossed over successfully to the other realm. This was my first time to set off motions to leave the body.

Thereafter, I started floating in a supine position going backwards, but not in my bedroom. This was also the first time when I was able to induce a crossover. While I was floating backwards, I specifically wanted to go to the Guanyin Temple. Instead, I was traveling through space, seeing very large flying objects like space stations. I also saw extraterrestrial beings in a room. They resembled slightly to humans. I even told myself that they were aliens.

Before long, I was following a person whom I knew down a hallway, telling myself that I was dreaming. I told myself to touch something to feel the sensation. I ran my right hand along the wall and the sensation was real.

Apparently, I was not satisfied with the current scene. I still wanted to go to the Guanyin Temple. So, I stretched out my arms and started spinning. Everything changed right away. I gradually showed up at another place that looked like a busy marketplace in China.

I once again wanted to change the scene. So, I spun and ended up in the middle of a busy boulevard like the Times Square. I opened my eyes with my hands, and I saw brighter and more colors to the people around. There was a kid making me upset for taking my slippers. I said to myself that I should not be angry. At that time, I wanted to bail out and wake up. I remembered to just fall asleep. I woke up at 7:30 am. It was a long 40' session.

032-121910
IMAGE OF TIME

My soul at times didn't know what to show in the mirror.

After 45' of meditation, I went back to nap at 7:06 am. No vibrations, just very subtle signals before I started floating around the room. I had to tell myself to calm down because I was somewhat stirred up. This was the first time I set the alarm for the session after meditation. So, I wouldn't know how I would react to the alarm going off.

When my floating stopped, I was facing down the floor at the right side of the bed, hovering but not touching the floor. I asked myself when this was over, shouldn't I return to my body's sleeping position. Suddenly, it felt like something lifted me from behind and slowly tossed me forward like a torpedo headfirst through the glass door.

At another busy scene, I was no longer floating. I saw a large tractor like vehicle. I also saw very large tree stumps and buildings with undefined black windows. I came across couple middle-aged women. I asked them what city it was. They looked at me but wouldn't say anything. I said, "Shang-hai?" and still no response.

Then I ended up inside an indoor mall. I flew inside and hovering under the ceiling. I saw a few people jumping in front of a large mirror. When I stood in front of the mirror, I couldn't see myself at all. At that moment, I tried to force myself through the mirror but that didn't work. I woke up at 7:29 and the alarm was set at 7:30.

HENRY C WONG

033-010811
MY CHILDHOOD FRIEND

My soul never ever loses all the loved ones.

After an hour of meditation, I was feeling alert and energized. I went back to bed at 6:57 am and lying on my left side. Shortly after, the subtle signal came. At around the same time, my wife was coughing in the living room. I thought it might interfere with the crossover. Nevertheless, I maintained my sleeping position and waited.

When the motions to leave the body started, I felt I was drooling. When I took off straight up the "Superman" style, I still felt the drooling around my mouth. Conversely, I was floating around the room with my feet dragging on the floor, wall and bed. Moreover, I did not see my sleeping body in bed.

After a while, I wanted to do something different. I went with the "torpedo" style, headfirst to the glass door at the foot of the bed. I said that I wanted to see Thousand-Hand Thousand-Eye Guanyin Bodhisattva. At that time, I did have reservation that I might not be able to go through the glass. But even so, I went ahead anyway through the glass door into a scene of animation and cartoon like characters.

Since I didn't get to see Guanyin Bodhisattva and nothing else was going on, I spun couple times to change the scene. The old scene froze up like a picture and the new scene was not yet defined. At that moment, I asked to see my childhood friend with whom I had lost contact for many years. It worked. This was the first time for me to specify a person to see.

My friend was coming through the door carrying something and there was a bed in front of her. I went over to talk to her. She looked young about thirty something, as pretty as I had always remembered of her. Her facial appearance was vivid and in high definition. She said that I was supposed to meet her at "Hyatt Gateway" and she didn't see me. She was also complaining about her G.I. not feeling well.

Then she walked out of the door into a bakery. I followed her and getting very close to her. I was staring at her face, and she was quiet. I asked her for her age, but she didn't answer me. But I was thinking in the 30s.

Surprisingly, I saw another one of me, a young good-looking guy in the 30s sitting and leaning in the bed talking to her. I couldn't hear what they were saying. I went back to stare at her face again. I felt so attracted to her that I wanted to look at her for a little longer.

At that time, I thought of going back to tell my older son about her. I knew full well that I couldn't bring this up to my wife. While I was still focusing on her, it all slowly faded away and I woke up at about 7:19 am. The session was 22' long.

Note: Before going back to bed, I specifically chose Thousand-Hand Thousand-Eye Guanyin Bodhisattva and my childhood friend to see in this session. Furthermore, I do not know any place with the name, Hyatt Gateway.

034-011111
MY PREVIOUS LIFE

Afterlife was simply just a pit stop for my soul.

After my 4 hours of regular sleep, I meditated for an hour. Afterwards, I went back to bed at 6:16 am and I specifically wanted to see my previous life and also my wife in my previous life.

Initially, I drifted into a state of unconsciousness before awakened to a blurry scene with some unknown people. I asked for more clarity, and it did become more and more clear.

I didn't know when I left my body with my feet leaving first. I only found myself just crouching next to the base of the glass door at the foot of my bed. Slowly, I was pressing myself against the glass. As I was going through the glass, I asked to see my previous life.

The scene seemed to be back in time to possibly the WWII era. I was walking with a blanket draping over me. I saw Asian soldiers all over the place and I knew they were Japanese. One came towards me shouldering a long rifle and he had a single star on his uniform. The setting was rural. He passed by me, and I was surprised he didn't stop me.

Before long, I was being escorted by two soldiers apparently to another location. One asked the other if I spoke Cantonese or English. They were speaking Cantonese. I asked one of them for the current year. He said he didn't know. I asked in Cantonese with a heavy accent. I didn't wait around. I flew high up and looked back at them from afar with such a joy.

As I was flying away, I asked to see my wife in my previous life. Shortly after, I turned up in bed being intimate with a woman. Presumably she was my wife. Although it felt so real, part of me knew that I was still sleeping alone somewhere else. I couldn't be sure if she was my current wife. However, I got the impression that was her even though I didn't get to see her face. Gradually, it all faded away and I woke up at 6:46 am. It was a 30' session.

035-012911
LOOKING FOR 3 SUNS

The cosmos is just as lively as my soul.

After 60' of meditation, I went back to bed at around 6:30 am. My wife was still in bed. Quickly, I settled down and lay on my left side. There was no vibration. Nevertheless, I sensed the subtle signal and directed my attention to it. Then I slowly left my body and moved around in the room. I was hovering up high overlooking my wife in bed, but I couldn't see my own body. I got restless because nothing was happening. I tried to fly up but hitting the ceiling instead.

There were two girls coming into the room. I chatted a little with one of them. I remembered telling myself that I needed to prepare myself better on what to do in the other realm, instead of just waiting around.

Finally, I opened the glass door and walked outside. It was raining and there was vine like plants everywhere. I flew up and tried to break through the vines in the rain. When I got above the vines, I saw the cosmos, stars and galaxies all around me. I verbally asked for more clarity and brightness. The universe did get brighter. I was just hovering out there. I was looking for the brightest spot where the sun was. I was also looking for 3 suns, turning full 360 degrees to scan the universe. I remembered if I could see 3 suns, then I must have transcended time and attained synchronicity.

Suddenly, I had this thought of seeing my childhood friend again. I turned up in a place but the woman there wasn't her. I chatted with her and others. Slowly, all faded away and I woke up. It had been 45 minutes.

036-013011
PURPLE SPACESHIP

Striking resemblance to Dunhuang Mogao Grottoes...

After an hour of meditation, I went back to bed. I felt the subtle signal but no vibrations. It just happened. I came straight out of my body riding with a solid purple color spaceship. I couldn't feel the existence of my body. Just my consciousness was traveling with the spaceship. I could see the front of the spaceship.

There was this loud noise as we were moving through space. We flew very close along the face of a massive sheer cliff where many grottoes situated. I could see clearly people living in those individual dwellings, although they seemed very small. The spaceship picked a spot and slowly parked into one of the grottoes. I was also chatting with the people inside before I woke up.

037-020111
IMAGES FROM BEYOND

My soul could remember a lot better than my mind.

After an hour of morning meditation, I went back to bed. I felt the subtle signal but no vibrations. Quickly after, I was out of my body and started roaming around the bedroom. When I pressed myself against the glass door at the foot of my bed, I was hoping to get through to another place. With some struggling, I got through the glass.

I ended up in a place full of vertical pillars of different shapes and designs. I also saw different figures and images on the surfaces of the pillars. They all looked very distinctive at the time, but I couldn't remember them. After looking at them for a while, I felt the scene was breaking up. I tried to spin to get to another scene, but it was too late. I woke up and yet remained calm and still. Thereafter, I drifted in and out of merely ordinary dreams.

038-020711
INCOHERENT SCENES

It is what it is...

After 40' of meditation, I went back to bed. I had no memory of any vibrations or movements. My wife was in the bedroom talking to me. Everything was very vivid. There was a 10-speed bike by the bed. I knew it didn't belong there and that caused me to doubt the reality of the scene.

Shortly after, I woke up to my apparent real left side sleeping position but still not quite sure. I didn't really want to wake up, so I kept still and began having the motions to leave the body. Directly after, I was resting on the floor next to the bed. I was complaining of the open window and bright light coming in, interfering with my travel.

The clock showed 8:22 am and I knew I was already late to work. I tried to make a call with a phone which didn't work. At that time, my wife was cooking in another room and my sister was at the bedroom door.

Gradually, I woke up clocking at only 7:22 am. Although everything in this session seemed so confusing, the experience was vivid.

039-021411
TAKE ME TO THE MOON

My soul can keep vivid and memorable images until the mind takes over.

After an hour of meditation starting from 5:10 am, I felt tired and groggy. I went back to bed and lay flat on my back. Vibrations were very strong, and I didn't mind at all. Actually, I felt very relaxed. I floated up swiftly in a supine position and spun around and around.

When the spinning stopped, I didn't want to stay around in the room. I asked, "Take me to the moon". Instantaneously, I flew straight up at hypersonic speed. But before getting anywhere, I was slowly waking up. As I was getting back into my body, I could still see the image of flying with debris whizzing by. I continued with more dreams afterwards.

040-021911
FLYING WITH A GIRL

Dreaming is merely a name that has no effects on the soul.

Hour long meditation seemed very short this morning. My left nostril was congested but no runny nose. I went back to bed afterwards. I felt the subtle signal but no vibrations. Immediately after, I was lifted out of my body and started floating in a supine position around the room.

The room was different from all the others that I had experienced before. It was bright and surrounded with glass windows which could see the outside. I was standing and hovering around the bed, but I didn't see my body.

Peeping through my half-closed eyelids, there were some patterns in my line of sight. They were randomly arranged short blue lines which reminded me of patterns on a Chinese antique vase.

While I was walking around impatiently, I saw a damaged fruit in bed, and I moved it to a shelf. I shouted, "I am dreaming. Everything is clear just like lucid dreams". Then I asked to be taken to see my mother, but it didn't work.

Then there was a girl of about 12 years old appeared in the room. We were holding hands and flew together out of that room. During the flight, I saw many large, complexed building structures with vibrant colors and amusement park like fixtures. Each independent building resembled to a boat.

We were very high up and couldn't see any beings. We both landed at a dark foreign place. There were men walking towards us, seemingly stopping us from going further. Slowly I woke up from that scene.

041-041811
MY DEAR TWO SONS

Without someone special in my soul, afterlife seems random and aimless.

After a short 30' meditation, I went back to bed. No vibrations but the out of body phase was quick, instant and definite. As soon as I was out of the body, I was at the foot of my bed anxious to fly away. I thought of my childhood friend but bounced back off the ceiling.

I was hovering from the ceiling looking down to my bed but found no body of mine. I approached the glass door in front of the bed and attempted to squeeze through the glass but failed. However, I remembered that it worked during my out of body experience on 03/30/2011.

I drew the curtains, and I saw my older son in his early teens playing sports with others. I was very excited, emotional and I screamed out something. I also saw him talking to my shirtless younger son who was also in his early teens.

042-061511
WHO'S FLYING

My soul can experience with or without a body.

I committed myself today not to desire to go anywhere. After an hour of meditation, I went back to bed. Vibrations came and the out of body phase followed. This time, I would just passively flow with the course of my experience.

While I paused a little standing next to my bed, I took off straight up at warp speed. However, I didn't have the feeling of my body flying as before. There was no sensation of my body, just my consciousness blasting off.

Shortly after, I was back looking at the design patterns of my bed cover. It was short medium blue strips on white. I remembered telling myself that I don't own anything like that in my real physical world. I woke up and drifted into unconscious dreams.

043-061611

GOING THROUGH THE WALL

Perception is reality, this saying also applies in the afterlife.

After an hour of meditation, I went back to bed. Vibrations and the out of body phase came. But this time, my two feet lifted and I was traveling in a supine position. I got a view of my feet in the front. My feet and legs were covered with the same blue strips patterns as mentioned yesterday.

I was floating around the room at first. When I reached the wall at the right side of the bed, I stopped and paused. It felt like someone else was controlling the whole thing, to see if my composure was maintained. As soon as I calmed myself down further, my feet went through the wall into another scene. I saw people fighting as in old ancient movies.

When I stood up, I felt someone holding me up from behind. He then came around to my front to talk to me, but I couldn't remember exactly what we said. I woke up thereafter.

044-062011

BLESSING LOS ANGELES

My soul can literally take compassion along to the afterlife.

After 50' of meditation, I went back to bed. Vibrations came and the out of body phase followed. I found myself out of breath at the end of the phase. Right away, I went back into my body.

But I kept myself still and felt the subtle signal coming again. This time, I didn't experience the out of body phase. I found myself up in the sky hovering but not flying anywhere. Through the scattered clouds, I saw a city with lights as if I was looking down at Los Angeles from a plane. The city was vast extending full 360 far into the horizon.

At the time, I recited the 9words Mantra in thought only. I couldn't remember whether I recited the Mantra out loud. At first, I was also extending my arms out with open palms directing the blessing to the city, while I was reciting the Mantra. Then I changed my open hands into the Dharma Seal.

After a while, I showed up in a city but nothing much was going on. I was hoping to change the scene by spinning but to no avail. The scene became less clear, and I drifted into a false awakening where the clock showed 1:30 pm. I thought that was not right. It should be 7 something in the morning before work, thereby I must not have woken yet. So, I walked out and flew away until I woke up. It had been a 30-minute session.

045-070111
HIMALAYAS TOP

Train, scenery, hilltop, Himalayas, people and emotions...
enough to bring on a feeling of nostalgia.

After 60'of meditation, I went back to bed. It took a while for me to settle in. I wasn't very tranquil. Once I felt being composed, I thought of leaving my body. It just happened. Instantly, I floated around the room with my feet in the front, gliding on the floor by the side of the bed. I said to myself that this feeling is very real.

When I approached the glass door, I was happy seeing nice scenery outside. I was certain that I would leave the room to another place. Directly after, I saw tall trees and beautiful scenery, as I was cruising by slowly. It was like being in a train looking out from a window. I saw houses all built on the hilltops. I noticed these houses are quite strange looking, not the kind that I knew. I tried to focus on the details of the houses.

Suddenly, I heard an announcement from a man's voice, "Himalayas Top". Thereafter, I arrived at that place, walking down a path with people around. For whatever reasons, I was moved and wept. The funny thing was that I was also wondering if my physical body in bed would be tearing up. I was also having food with people and mingling with them.

When it became uneventful, I faded away from that place into another scene before I woke up. It was another 30 minutes session.

Note: I have never been to the Himalayas.

046-070311
LEFT EYE SEEING

Afterlife is not a dark place...but blazing bright light abounds.

After 60' of meditation, I went back to bed. The first out of body phase was terminated when I was feeling out of breath after leaving my body. The second time around, I simply just thought of leaving my body. Shortly, I started floating supinely with feet in front. I was roaming from room to room exceedingly fast.

I was looking at a scene appeared like a large picture, under very dim light. I told myself to open my eyes. When opened, everything became bright but blank. Then I would try again with only my left eye open. And this time, I saw the same scene bright and clear. There were many lively cute small monkeys moving all over the place. It reminded me of Monkey King. I remembered telling myself that my right brain controlled my left eye.

047-071411
MAJESTIC SCENERY

The sensation of pain and discomfort also exists in the afterlife.

After 2 hours of meditation, I went back to bed lying on my left side. It was nice and quiet. There was no signal initially and I just fell asleep. I remembered focusing on being composed and the out of body phase happened.

Before long, I floated off without any prior vibrations. When I looked at my bed, I once again saw the familiar scattered blue strips patterns on my bed covers. I also saw the very same patterns and some other images of various unrecognizable figures. They were all over the transparent curtains draping over the glass doors. I did recognize the image of an elephant. I tried hard to concentrate in discerning the figures.

After twisting and turning all over the room, I slowly descended to the floor. As soon as I realized that I had the thought, "Am I being taken to hell?" I immediately started reciting the 9words Mantra. While I was floating, I experienced pain on the right side of my rib cage. As I was gradually waking up, I realized I was holding my breath and gasping for air.

Before long, I found myself playing with some kind of toy car and felt someone elbowed me in my back. I turned around and looked to the right, finding myself in my bed with my younger son in his tween. He was laughing and I was pushing him off my bed, thinking that he elbowed my back. As he was about to fall off the bed, I heard my wife in the bathroom next door. She walked out looking a little bigger and different. I felt her body and noticed some differences.

As I looked over the room, I tried to open my eyes to see better but concerned it might fade away faster. Once opened, everything got so much brighter and vivid. I told myself that this is as real as it comes and as real as the physical one.

My wife and I walked out to a large open patio area that I had never seen before. I asked her what city we are in, but she didn't answer. I had a panoramic view of the ocean with majestic rocky islands jutting out of the water everywhere. I was quite taken by the view, and it slowly faded away from me. This long session took only 30 minutes.

048-071611
UNIVERSALITY OF EMPATHY

Mantra works way better than weapons in the afterlife.

After 2 hours of meditation, I went back to bed at around 7:08 am. I was quite alert at the time. I was lying on my left. There was no vibration or out of body movement.

Eventually, I was awakened to a place where I was crawling and struggling. I pushed my hands forward and I started moving much faster. Shortly after, I was flying from room to room, seeing people eating at their tables. I got myself stuck at a window where I wanted to fly away. I was struggling to break free from the strings of a curtain. After breaking free, I was able to hover only few feet off the ground. There were a lot of people watching me and also wanted to hover.

While I was walking into a room, there were 3 shady characters following me. I knew they wanted to do me harm and I didn't recite the 9words Mantra. Instead, I was trying to think of a box cutter in my right hand and attempted to cut a guy's neck. That didn't work and I wanted to bail out of that scene. One of them was holding me down while the whole scene was fading away. It still took a while before I broke away.

Arriving at a new scene, I was walking up a large flight of stone stairs. There was a very large sign at the top with some markings like the Chinese characters. I tried to decipher what they were.

From here onto another scene, I was moving a large piece of board by myself while another guy was moving some bricks and board. He was asking for help because things around him were collapsing. My friend didn't do anything but just standing by. I got my hands full and couldn't help. The collapse continued around that guy. He fell through level after level to far below until he couldn't be seen. All I could see were small dots where clusters of people frantically rescuing others buried in the collapse. Even so, water came and swept over all of them. I was saddened with tears and slowly woke up. Session lasted for 30 minutes.

049-072411

BLIND FAITH IN MYSELF

<hr>

My soul enjoys a challenge of its faith...

After 40'of meditation, I felt relaxed, soothing and light. I went back to bed and thought of leaving my body. Although my wife was sleeping right next to me, I still crossed over.

Moment later, I was tidying up my own things while people arguing in another room. My white shoes got wet when I was walking down a flooded street. I regretted that I didn't have my boots on.

As I was approaching the intersection, everything was unfamiliar to me. I saw some kind of machine control at the pedestrian walk. I decided to focus more on it so that I could stay in the scene longer. I might have been frustrated for some reasons. I started kicking and banging the machine to create a scene. Some people gathered around. I wanted to do something, to stir up something, or to cause something to happen.

Surprisingly, I found myself walking out to the traffic. I couldn't see any cars, but I could clearly hear fast moving vehicles whizzing past me, just like standing in the middle of a freeway. I didn't know why I would just keep walking out even though I could feel the vehicles zooming by me.

In that moment, I was not afraid or worried. I had this tremendous faith in me that I would not be harmed or getting hit. At that instant, I was carried and lifted out of that scene, floating and slowly rotating into a calm but unfamiliar room. I couldn't make out much of my surrounding. As I was staring at some patterns, the scene froze up and gradually faded away from me.

050-072911
A BEAUTIFUL TRAIN RIDE

The perception of time is simply the change of images.

After a comfortable 2 hours of meditation, I went back to bed at 7.10 am. My wife had already woken up. I cuddled with her for a while and joked about us getting old and stiff. After this interruption, I didn't think I would be sleepy at all. Nevertheless, the out of body phase started anyway without vibrations.

Suddenly, I found myself in an unfamiliar bedroom. As I was floating off my body, I felt my wife still touching me. I was wondering if I would take her along. After floating up high in the room, I even came down and bumped her a bit. She got up wanting to open the window. I said to myself, "Oh no, I would certainly wake up." Quite the opposite, everything was much brighter.

I saw flowers growing and blossoming like what you would see in a speed up time lapse video. It was not static but constantly changing, as if I was looking out of a moving train's window. Images were continuously passing by. I wanted to stick my feet out of the window. I was also anxious to go somewhere else. When my toes barely touched the outside through the window, I saw small vivid flowers swiftly formed and blossomed at the tip of my big toes. Once the flowers and vegetation filled up the outside of the window, I told myself that it would be hard to get through.

Next, I showed up in a small town, not a village, with my wife. The name of that place was clearly written out as two Chinese characters which mean heaven and earth. From that point on, I gradually woke up to 7:38 am.

051-073011
DANCING TO THE BEAT
OF THE UNIVERSE

My soul does not know why this or that...

After a pleasant meditation, I was running late and no time to nap. But my legs and feet felt strained, tired and sore. So, I went back to bed. In no time at all, the out of body movements started. Before I was completely settled at the end of the out of body phase, I felt I was holding my breath. But this time, I stopped the holding and started breathing in and out. Surprisingly, I didn't get pulled back into my physical body.

I was floating and gliding all over the room, with such grace and smoothness not seen before. There was also a nice music playing at the same time. I could see my feet together dancing in the air everywhere.

Although I was aware of myself being in my room, the background looked exactly like the dark universe with specks of stars everywhere. When I approached the curtain, I wanted to take off to go somewhere else. Then I felt my wife touching me, caused me to wake up right away.

This time, I kept still and tried to focus on my mind. I saw a live universe with its moving galaxies and constellations.

That image lasted for only a short time, about 10 seconds at most. Then it all went dark as usual. Nevertheless, I was still able to see the glowing silhouette of that lively image right before I woke up. All lasted only 10 minutes, but I was late to work. My legs felt good, and my mind was clear.

052-080811

CRASHING THROUGH THE ATRIUM

My soul's European connection...

After meditation, I went back to bed lying on my left side. I felt the subtle signal. So, I concentrated and held still but the out of body phase was not detected. It happened very fast. I found myself looking up and watched, large square frames crashing through the glasses of a tall glass atrium. They came down with a loud bang right onto me. I was stunned but not afraid. Immediately after that crash, I also saw these long rods with 90 degrees short spikes crashing down before it all quieted down.

I was looking at a wall of European ornaments. The wall was not flat but decorated with uneven designs. I was looking at it quite closely. There was no place for me to spin to change the scene. As I opened my eyes, I felt my glasses coming off obstructing my view, thereby causing the scene to fade away.

It was 9:00 am and I was late to work. I was asking my teenage daughter and her younger brother, both of whom I didn't recognize, if they were late. They said no. I had to hop into a taxi with only my socks on. I was trying to close the door while I was driving into a congested street of an open market. Someone called the police who was questioning me for stealing the taxi. The session was about 30 minutes long.

053-080911
A MESSAGE FROM MY SONS

If there's a message meant for my soul to see, it'll be unmistakably clear.

After meditation, I went back to bed. There was an itch in my left foot keeping me from staying still. Eventually, the out of body phase still ensued. I got out of my body and floated off to the right side of the bed.

Then I turned around and looked at the bed. I saw a small person sleeping under the cover looking back at me. It was not my wife, and I was a bit startled. I proceeded to float up and across the bed again to the left side. At that time, I wanted to go somewhere else, but I didn't really know where to go. So, I just flowed with it, wherever it would take me.

When I looked across the bed, I saw my younger son in his toddler age, peeping around, smiling and laughing. He extended his hand to me. I didn't know if I was able to use my hand or to hold anything. I extended my hand, this time it looked like a real hand, to hold his. I was pulling him towards me, but he was trying to hide behind something like a large pillow. Suddenly, he became my older son in about the same age and laughing. He had some line markings on his forehead. He was speaking to me in Mandarin. He said something about me being qualified and need to take elderly

Mr. Xu to do volunteer work together. When he said "Xu", that Chinese character appeared unmistakably, as a clear image right in front of me.

At that moment, I remembered saying that I had been told the same, in the night dreams before my meditation this morning. I was so deeply moved. I broke down and really cried while my older son was looking on. While I was crying, I noticed his body's interior image seemed mechanical. Slowly I woke up and still had tears in my physical eyes.

054-081411
SEEING WITHOUT KNOWING

Just amazed how much more my soul gets to see...

After 2 hours of meditation, I went back to bed and gave my wife a hug. That didn't affect anything thereafter. Without signals and vibrations, I found myself floating around in the room. This time I was standing upright and hovering off the floor. I did desire to go somewhere else but didn't know where.

Suddenly, I started to recite the 9words Mantra in the direction of the bed. I also stretched out my two hands with Dharma Seal directing at the bed. There was nobody over the bed at that moment. A circular image about the size of a softball appeared over where I was aiming. It also displayed colorful wavelike strands moving and changing within the circle. But there were no rays of light from my hands to the target. Slowly I also visualized a very abstract colorful figure next to the circle.

Shortly, I got this feeling of a familiar signal that I was about to go somewhere else. In a flash, I was at a window counter in an agency office. I was looking through the opening over a counter. A woman was about to turn around towards me. I was wondering if she would be someone that I knew. She turned out not someone I recognized. She had curly hair and facial acne. Again, as usual, I asked her what city we were in. She might have said something, but I didn't catch it.

Then I went through the door into a large office space with a lot of people working. I asked them the same question and they told me in Mandarin. I couldn't understand what they said. Moment after, I just woke up. The session lasted only 15 minutes.

055-081511
NUMBER 11

My soul knows all about me and much more...

After meditation, I went back to bed, and I told myself to look out for the number 11 in the other realm. The vibrations and the out of body phase were very quick and brief. I floated a little bit before getting stuck face down at a corner.

As the image slowly faded away in front of me, my stillness led me to another scene in a large auditorium. I still remembered to look for the number 11. Up high, I saw a large a totem that looked roughly like the Chinese character "Hua" meaning magnificent. At that moment, I was thinking my actual life was somewhere back in the real world.

Afterwards, I was just dancing away by myself with music playing, in front of other people. Slowly, my dancing took off into the air. I took a leap with confidence and faith off a cliff, flying across a landscape of lava rock below me. Gradually, I dropped down and landed on the rocky ground.

I was walking along an alley in a town. I heard noises behind me closing in. When I tried to fly up, I ran into all sorts of obstacles above me. I became trapped in a room. A woman I didn't know was helping me. I tried to go through layers of windows before they caught up with me. Then I just stay put until the scene changed. Thereafter, I went through two separate false awakenings before waking up. The session was 30 minutes long.

056-081611

STRETCHING THE IMAGINATION

---

*My soul remembers the pain and suffering in
the physical body.*

I was anxious to get out of the meditation although I had no
discomfort. After meditation, there were still a lot of disturbances from my wife before I went back to bed. Apparently,
her disturbances from the bathroom didn't affect me after
all. There was no vibration, just that subtle signal. In a flash, I
found myself floating in the room. Right after I realized I was
floating; I could still hear my wife's noise in the bathroom.

I started instructing myself to rise upward with no problem. When I asked to go out of the room, I quickly changed
to a supine position with my my feet pointing straight out in
front. At the glass door, there was a transparent elastic mem-
brane over the glass door. My feet pushed out only enough
to stretch it, thereby I didn't get to go out.

In the next scene, I was walking as a normal human being on the ground. While moving around, I was able to see
my arms and legs. I clearly remembered that I had sore left
elbow and painful right shoulder in my physical body. When
I bent my elbows, I could feel the tightness in the tendons
and the limited flexibility. I started putting some pressure on

them causing them to bend. They slowly became more flexible and allowed more range of motion without any pain.

Then I wondered if I could stretch out my stiff hamstrings as in my physical body. I squatted down and stretched out the left leg, tight at first then it got loosened up. There were several chickens pecking around me. The scene faded away before I could stretch my right leg. I woke up and my body apparently was still the same without any detectable changes.

057-081911
THE FACE SHIFTER

Synchronicity is when images appear randomly with no apparent connections.

After meditation, my wife left for work right before I went back to bed. As soon as I began the out of body movements, she came in to follow me floating around the room. Then on the other hand, I knew full well that she had already left the house.

I hovered vertically up high and charged towards her face with my feet. She made some noise and morphed into another face that I didn't recognize. But she did not back away. She came towards me and grabbed ahold of me. Out of fear and panic, I burst out the 9words Mantra continuously. She did become more subdued but still no retreat. I even thought of Amitafo Buddha and Guanyin Bodhisattvas.

She wanted to feel my belly and asked about the baby. By then, she already became a clearly defined person, a female in her 30s. I said to myself that if I ever saw her somewhere in the physical world, I would definitely recognize her. She went on to say something about her husband carrying a baby. Shortly, a machine somehow went over her and pinned her down to the floor. The she was gone from the scene.

After that, I ran away into another room where there was enough space for me to spin for another scene. I spun for quite a while to make sure that the scene would change. I arrived at a mall where lots of people and kids gathered. I walked through the crowd and ended up climbing the stairs.

Someone was restraining me to an eye examination chair with all kinds of machines. He said something about increased recognition capacity and cornea. But I asked him if this is a restaurant. Before long, things froze up and slowly faded away before I woke up from these 20 minutes session.

058-082611
BLESSINGS FOR ALL

In the state of synchronicity, deeds of compassion would be instantaneously received.

My wife was out of town. After the meditation, I went back to bed at 7:00 am. I was lying on my usual position to the left. Initially, I was just drifting in and out of unconsciousness. When I became awakened, vibrations came fast. Without a pause, I flew straight up into the open space. I wanted to have my eyes wide open to marvel the surrounding scene which was vividly bright and colorful.

There were countless worldly beings below while I was hovering. I prayed for blessings upon all of them, by the virtue of my recitation of the 9words Mantra and both of my Dharma Seal. This was something that I had set out to do, instead of trying to figure out who to see or where to go.

I was approaching closely to a huge ship like aircraft. I also could see people on it. I felt its gravity pulling me in, preventing me from flying away. I struggled to pull away as that big aircraft moved and turned.

In the next scene, I was at a factory of some kind. They made all kinds of top to toes suits, like cold water diving suits. I also asked them what the brand was, and they said something unknown to me. Moment after, I walked into another city. I saw couple giants, friendly and not hostile. I woke up with clarity, feeling fresh and energized. Session was about 30 minutes long.

059-082911
SOCIAL GATHERINGS

Happy soul brings about happy scenes. ‾‾‾‾‾‾‾

After meditation, I went back to bed. There was no vibration or out of body movement. I just instantly found myself hovering and floating in a large cafeteria. There were a lot of people gathering. They could touch me while I was hovering. Nothing much was happening, so I flew to a large platform on top of a building. From there I started spinning hoping to go somewhere else. I had this thought, "Change the scene." At that moment, I was full of joy and happiness. While I was spinning, I said my childhood friend's name again.

The next scene was at a party with a lot of people around. I just knew it was an open house of some business held by my wife's old friend. It was next to an Indian restaurant and a Chinese store. I saw the opening date being Aug 1 and 7:00 pm. I was very excited thinking that I had traveled to the future.

From the outside of the party, I heard someone calling me, "What are you doing here?" I went over and I knew it was my wife, but that woman had a very short sassy hairdo and a different face. Shortly after, she changed to a kid, then a man. I asked him, "How long had you known me?" He said something like 16-18 years. Up to this point, everything in all the scenes were so real, bright and colorful. I even made that comment to myself.

Then we walked together to the back where there was a dark alley. There were another two guys approaching us. I felt being cornered in and threatened. I just flew away and intended to go all the way back. However, I did go through one more short scene before waking up. It was a 20-minute session.

060-090211
YEAR 1556

Time somehow brings about strong sentiment to my soul.

After meditation, since my wife was still sleeping, I went back to nap on the floor mat in my study room. There was a disturbing cold breeze over my head and face. I couldn't get it going flat on my back. So, I turned to my left side with something blocking the cold.

I felt myself rising above tall buildings right at the transition state, but it didn't last. And I turned over to my right side with less breeze. Without the discomfort from cold, I started to settle in. Hence, the vibrations and the out of body movements swiftly ensued.

Soon after, I found myself floating in a unfamiliar room. I peeped through the horizontal blinds out of the window. I saw my wife but not clearly at a bus stop shelter, which was covered with green ivy. When I looked further down the street to the left, I saw tall brick buildings as in the east coast cities of United States. To the right, there was more open area but still looked like the inner city.

While I was walking around the apartment, I felt the scene was about to fade. I spoke out, "Brighter, clearer, stabilize." I really wanted to stay in that scene. It worked. It got more clear and brighter. The scene just settled down and became more fulfilled.

I was happy and ran around the place to check out things and clues. I came across a calendar on the wall. I flipped through the pages, and I couldn't make any sense out of those foreign symbols and numbers. But I did see something like 1556. I also asked my wife's sister what the year was. She said six. I said, "You meant 1556." When I asked her, "Where are we?" She pointed it out on a map and said, "Queens." I also felt her husband in the background. We were all talking about a man named Dan who was supposed to be my wife's husband. When I had to leave, I broke down in tears, telling them that I was from the future. I told myself that I might never see them again.

I walked into another room to a tight spot next to a crib, rushing into a spin. Apparently, they went to get more friends to see me. I was thinking, "I don't want it to be a freak show." The spin didn't work because I was hitting things around me. So, I went over to the other side of the crib to spin. Everything just faded away. I found myself still in tears and about to walk into the bathroom to tell my wife what happened in my dream. But instead, I woke up in my study room. It was a long one-hour session.

061-091411
A SCIENCE FIELD TRIP

My soul was hustling in this journey...

Today my hour meditation seemed like only 30 minutes. Right before the 60' alarm went off, I was seeing images and myself spinning a big broken egg with another guy. My state of mind was a little strange at the time.

I went back to nap again on the floor mat in my study room, since my wife was still sleeping in the bedroom. It was already very bright right before 8:00 am. I took on my usual sleeping position. There was no vibration or out of body movement.

Suddenly, I found my wife coming into my room. She rolled up a blanket right in front of me while I was still lying on the floor mat. I was quite upset and argued with her, complaining that she shouldn't come in to disturb me. While I was talking to her, she morphed into a bald head man with an evil look. There were blood vessels appearing all over his face. I told her to look at herself in the bathroom mirror.

Shortly after, I woke up and still in my usual sleeping position. I kept still expecting to continue with it. This time, I rolled to the left until facing down. In a flash, I popped up and hovered in the middle of the room. I remembered that I didn't want to hang around the room for too long. So, I started to spin in midair for the first time. Even after I stopped spinning, the surrounding would continue spinning.

Eventually, a new scene arrived. I was running on a street seeing rats in a pothole. When I was out in the open, I immediately wanted to find out any signs of a foreign land, such as two suns. I looked at the sky from one end of a wide and long boulevard to the other end. From afar I saw massive smoke like clouds from the ground up to the sky. Again, I remembered not to linger around for too long in any scene, which could lead to premature awakening.

I spun again and showed up somewhere in a university hallway. I was checking to see if this little bell-shaped object obeyed the law of gravity. There were several of them. I used my finger to pop one upward and it slowly fell back down to the surface. It suspended in air when I touched it. They all seemed to be hovering rather.

As I continued walking down the hallway, I saw large dinosaurs at the end of it. I walked past them and wanted to move on to the next scene. This time, spinning didn't bring anything. I knew it was time to get back and wake up. I remembered to just relax, sit tight and take a nap before waking up. Another long session of 45 minutes.

062-092611
SOUTHERN CALIFORNIA

The true existence is inconceivably broader than the physical universe.

Due to the colder temperature, I had a sore throat and little runny nose. During the hour of meditation, I recited the 9words Mantra and practiced energy exercises. It worked and I felt much better.

After the meditation, I went back to nap again on the floor mat in my study room, since my wife was still sleeping in the bedroom. I was lying on my left side, relaxed and still, with nothing to think about. I was just waiting for it to happen in a state of dead calm.

When I became awakened from a state of unconsciousness, I was in the transition state. The out of body movements started without vibrations. I rolled to the right and again getting stuck against the bookshelves next to the floor mat.

I didn't want to hang around there for too long, so I said, "Higher-Self". Immediately, swirling motion started around me. I showed up at a place where there were many of the large model trains in a large area. I took a close look at them and touched them. It was kind of dim and unclear. I asked for more clarity. It cleared up right away. After walking for a little while, I asked again for more clarity. It cleared up some more.

When I walked into someone's home in a building, I saw couple kids and I shook hands with one of them. The touch of her hand was warm and real. Later, more people came in and questioned me if I were the doctor they called for. I told them that I was a dentist, and they got the wrong person.

Thereafter, I walked out to the open. There were two people outside. I asked them, "Where is this place? Downtown L.A.?" One of them said, "Southern California." Then I asked them what year. They didn't say anything.

I continued walking down the street. I decided to just pop into a Korean restaurant to see if there were any people. There were people ready to serve me, but I left. I kept walking and felt the scene was fading. I ended up in a room with some people. I felt it was about to end. I even tried to focus on something to prolong the scene. I told myself to remember all. I went through another dream, and it took a while before I actually woke up.

063-100711
BODY SOUL MISALIGNMENT

_____

This is a case of the crash-landing equivalent of incarnation.

_____

After 45' of meditation, I felt alright going back to bed while my wife was still sleeping. Initially, I was on my back but switched to the left side. My body became really relaxed, calm and nearly nonexistent. I didn't really care my wife was right next to me under the same thick and warm bed covering. I just knew it would come. The subtle signal came when I was settled down completely with no thoughts.

Then without any vibrations, the out of body movements started. I rolled out of my body to the right onto my wife. I could even see her. She wasn't sleeping and seemed awake. Quickly after, I stood up and pulled myself straight back away from the bed.

A while later, I saw my wife walking out of the room and I followed her to my study room. It was getting dark, and I asked for more clarity. It got brighter. When I bumped into her in the study, I recoiled back into my physical body in a flash.

Apparently, I felt her tugging on the bed covering at the time. It was one of those unexpected and abrupt termination of the out of body experience. While I was keeping still, I felt something not settling in my body. I just held still and slowly I got this comfortable feeling that everything was back into their right place again. I gradually started to move my body a little, and once again feeling energetic, relaxed and a sense of well being.

064-102511

AUTHENTIC REQUESTS

My soul responds to only genuine connections.

During an hour of meditation, my neck was very tired. I had to practice breathing exercise to energize myself and straighten my neck. Meditation went by quickly without thinking of anything.

After meditation, I went back to bed. I told myself to stay alert. While I stayed calm and immobile, I tried something different by shifting my awareness to the third eye area. Immediately, I got that subtle signal response. I was not aware of any vibrations or out of body movements.

Next thing I found myself in a dream where I questioned the validity of reality. I asked myself, "What do I need to do to tell if this is not real?" I envisioned myself being enveloped by white light. I asked couple times, "Take me to higher self" but nothing happened. Maybe I just rushed through it and didn't put enough effort in it.

Suddenly, I found myself floating supinely feet first, in a large room full of other people. I was able to direct my body up down left right and it would move accordingly. I was running through many corridors. Since there wasn't anything interesting, I spun for a change without any specific destinations. Before the spin, I did casually ask to be taken again to see my childhood friend. But that didn't work.

The spin landed me in a street where people were lifting heavy things. It was like a campus area. It seemed like I had been here before. I stopped a girl and asked her what's the name of the college. She said Yolander something college that I had never heard of. As I walked down a path away from the street, I became aware of myself being a traveler.

There was a suspicious guy approaching me. I didn't bother to find out. I just flew straight up and appeared in a room where my sister was also there. The clock showed 8:15. I said, "The whole thing took 45'."

Slowly, I woke up and the time was only 7:50. Session was about 30 minutes. Note: I went back to bed at 7:20 after meditation.

065-111111
GO WITH THE FLOW

The afterlife manifests scenes from my soul's cumulative experiences.

After 60' of meditation, I went back to bed. My wife wasn't home, and it was quiet. I tried to recreate the sinking feeling. After couple attempts, I felt a mild full body vibration. From that, I quickly rolled to the right. But I couldn't get out of the body. So, when I rolled back to the left too much, I ended up facing down.

After I got out of the body, I said, "Upright now" and I stood upright. I said, "Hovering now" and I rose up high with a bird's eye view of the house. I felt my eyes were shut with dried mucus. Meanwhile, I also asked for clarity. After a little struggle, everything got clear. I did wonder if I was seeing everything through my shut eyelids.

As I walked to another part of the house, it looked more like an apartment. I saw my wife sitting in a chair in a small kitchen. She didn't really look like her. I asked her if we had two sons. She said something like, "All four of us are in different orders, might mean in different worlds." I tried to ask her to explain.

Then I turned hyperactive walking around the apartment, feeling the touch of the wall. I also did a Chinese horse stance and slapping my own thighs.

Before long, I wanted to go somewhere else. I raised my right arm straight up and said, "Take me to Hong Kong." In a moment, I arrived at a large open area. It appeared as a lawless war zone. People were carrying rifles, riding small ATV vehicles and roaming all over the beach area. There were no buildings around. I woke up shortly after. Session was 20 minutes long.

066-121711
PROMISE KEPT

My soul knew about time of the physical world.

After 60' of meditation, I went back to bed at 7:00 am. I didn't set the alarm to go off at 7:30 am. But instead, I told myself to wake up at that time. Vibrations and out of body movements came while I was already in an unconscious dream state. It didn't even wait for me to be awakened at the transition state.

I floated around the room a bit before kneeling by the bed. I remembered to stabilize the scene first before doing anything else. First, I asked for clarity and then the entire scene in front of me cleared up and came alive. It became especially vivid but there was a different feel from before. Maybe it was because I never bothered to stabilize the scene in my room around my bed and body. I asked for more clarity couple more times to be sure.

Later, I found myself in a small shed, walking out into a crowded street with people and vehicles. There were Chinese characters everywhere and totems on vehicles and buildings. Yet I attempted to fly away but just not too far up.

Next, I found myself in another home setting where my younger son in his preteen was with me. I didn't take a good look at his face. We went to McDonald's and looked at one of those large menus displays. I was saying to myself, "They sure have different foods in this world."

I went on to dig through some newspaper, looking for the date. I thought I saw 2124 and said to myself, "That's over a hundred years from now and I'm from the past." I also saw some other languages and numbers look-alike, supposedly representing the date. This world must have a different system for calendar and time. When I saw my wife, I said to her, "I guess you're stuck with me again."

By that time, I felt I had been out for quite a while and wanted to go back. While I was washing my hands, my right hand turned dark. I said to my younger son that it was time to go. I was thinking of finding a corner to take a nap to go back.

But instead, I walked into another room with more open space, so that I could do my spin. At first, I was bumping into something during the spinning. As I spun faster, I felt I was taking off away from the scene back into my body. When I realized that it was the real awakening, I held still to recollect the details of the whole experience. When I was ready to move and open my eyes, I saw 7:29 on my clock.

067-123011
VISITING MY NEIGHBOR

Calling out a place to go to...

After meditation, I went back to bed. I slept from 7:11 to 7:34 am. As I was about to drift back into sleep, the out of body movements came. Right before I left my body, I heard noise from my wife entering the room and sleeping right next to me. Interestingly, I ignored all that and continued with my pursuit. I floated off to the glass door. At that instant, I told myself to fly to my back neighbor's house.

While I was flying, I remembered not to lose my focus and get distracted by anything else. When I got there, I heard people talking and saw couple persons at the dinner table. I looked around and asked for clarity. As I looked back at their yard, I saw a swimming pool and vaguely my house, which situated few feet below just like my physical house. I woke up to my mentally preset alarm at 7:40 am.

068-010712
MIRROR MIRROR

*Never know what facial image would appear
in the mirror of the afterlife.*

After meditation, I went back to bed around 6:30 am. I didn't think much of anything. I was lying on my usual left side position. Without any vibration, I drifted out of my body to the right. Strangely, I drifted back into my body and floated out once again to the left. I asked for clarity twice and the scene cleared up.

Once the scene stabilized, I wanted to go through the glass but not knowing where to go thereafter. I visualized my head through the glass, and it worked. But my body didn't follow through.

Shortly after, I went to my wife's bathroom. I didn't expect to see anybody in the mirror. I saw a deformed person not looking like me and not really a clear human face. At that time, my wife walked in, and I walked out. I opened the front door and wanted to take off to somewhere else. I was also concerned about the house alarm not being deactivated. Slowly I drifted back and woke up at 7:11 am.

069-012612
INTERMIXING OF IMAGES

Familiar images are intermingled with unknown scenes throughout the immaterial realm.

After meditation, I went back to bed lying on my left side. I heard my wife coming in during my out of body movements. I was thinking I could still do it with the distractions. I just popped out of my body to the left. As I looked back at my bed, I did not see my body.

My wife got up from her side. At that time, I asked for clarity and the scene got more vivid. She came towards me and wanted to give me a hug. I hugged her and then I wanted to go somewhere else.

I was looking out from an opening and saw many houses from a bird's eye view. Someone told me it's San Gabriel Valley.

While I was in another room, I noticed the black colored floor with a unique abstract design. I spun around but got nowhere. I also talked to some friends of my sons. The scene became blurry and not as clear as before. I woke up and realized my wife wasn't around at all.

070-013012
SUPERIMPOSED BODY

Seeing is always from the soul, but perspective can differ as in the physical body.

After a seemingly short one-hour long meditation, I went back to bed lying on my right side for a change. Without vibrations, only the out of body movements came. I just noticed that this time my left arm swung around from the right to 90 degrees straight up, as my body turned from right to left. I could see my left arm and hand in dark silhouette.

The seeing was no longer coming from the physical body but from the perspective of my nonphysical body itself. Before long, I was out and and moving around the room. Again, my wife was also in the room.

Everything seemed confusing because of two false awakenings. I asked to be taken to my "higher-self" but to no avail. I ended up somewhere else with people and places that I didn't know. Since I wrote this late in the evening, a lot of the vivid details faded away from my memory. Session was 20 minutes long.

071-021312
SLEEP PARALYSIS

Soul awakens, when body and mind fall asleep.

After meditation, I went back to bed lying on my left side because I just couldn't relax being flat on my back. Suddenly, I felt this shoving and tugging on my back, but I couldn't move at all, completely immobilized. I felt annoyed and fought against it, while I was reciting the 9words Mantra. It didn't go away. Then I found myself turning over to the right. I saw my wife, thinking it was too early for her to go to work.

I also started having the out of body movements, turning and rolling off the bed. I asked for clarity and the room became very vivid and real. As I strolled into another room, my wife walked past me without saying a thing.

I started feeling sluggish with no energy. I asked for more energy to no avail. I was not floating but touching the floor. Shortly in a false awakening, I was in bed and my wife also came in. Gradually, I woke up. The clock showed 7:29 and I did ask to be waked up at 7:30.

Note: My wife went to work very early and did not come to bed at all that morning.

072-022312
SECRET MESSAGE

Seeing is pointless without the associated wisdom.

After meditation, I went back to bed, but my mind was pre-occupied and not empty as usual. And I knew it would interfere with this morning's experience. So, I cleared up my mind and the out of body movements immediately followed.

Without vibrations, I took on a supine position and float-ed headfirst towards the glass door. During the process, my groin center felt a lot of pressure. My legs would straighten upward, and I floated upside down.

My eyes were closed but I still saw myself in a pajama pants that I didn't recognize. Then again, I said to myself, "You could see without your eyes." Thereby, I stopped pay-ing attention to my eyes. When I floated to the glass door, I went right through the glass with no problem.

Shortly after, I was looking up the sky and I saw count-less small things up there. I would also zoom in and focused on some of them individually. I saw scissors and man-made items, all suspended in the sky.

A while later, I felt a soft woman hand holding my left hand and then both of her hands on my hands. Going back into my bedroom, she just put both of her hands on my face and held it softly. Nevertheless, I couldn't see her face clearly. After I moved my head back, she articulated specifically eight Chinese words. She said it twice and asked me not to forget. I couldn't really understand the phrase and I also forgot the seventh character.

After that, I saw my sister in front of me, but she didn't really look like her. Nevertheless, I went over and wanted to touch her vivid face. I woke up instead. Session was 30 minutes long.

073-022512

I MUST BE DREAMING

Only referencing can provide insights to encountered images.

After meditation, I went back to bed and kept everything still. I got some mild vibrations but no obvious out of body movements. I didn't realize I had already drifted into unconscious dreams, until I wanted to check my cellphone for time. I pulled it off my wrist and I saw a large calculator like device. I said to myself, "This does not look like my phone at all. I must be dreaming."

Once I knew I was in a state of dreaming, I became a little bolder. I walked out to the open and immediately wanted to fly. But this time, my consciousness stretched and snaked around the roof overhang to the roof top. From there, I flew straight across in superman style to the horizon. I stalled and slowly dropped down to the ground. I just stayed there in those large grains of sand.

I opened my eyes, and I ended up in my bed with my head situated towards the foot of the bed. I also saw the ceiling recessed light turned on. At that point, I realized that I was not fully awakened because I rarely ever had the lights turned on. Slowly I woke up in this 15-minute session.

074-022712

WOMEN IN PICTURES

Without the physical experience...what's there to engage in the afterlife?

After meditation, I went back to bed lying in a composed position. Mild vibrations came and immediately subsided. I kept still and tried it again. Shortly, the out of body movements started. I rolled to the right and stood straight up out of my body.

I was hovering and floated to the bathroom. While looking down from high up, I concentrated on what I was seeing. I asked for clarity, and it got more vivid. At times, I descended and felt my feet touching the floor.

As I was moving from the bathroom to the bedroom, through the hallway into my study room, I couldn't recognize any of the items along the way. In the study room, I looked down at my meditation altar table but couldn't recognize any of it. I saw a large picture hanging on the wall of an unknown woman.

Then I came down to rest on the floor. I used hand signals to tell my younger son and two other kids, all preteens, to get out and leave me alone.

Before long, I woke up again only to see another smaller picture of a woman. When I noticed the altar was being placed against the side instead of the middle, I realized that I was still dreaming.

I got up and walked around. I saw my older son in his tween. I got a little choke up when I was holding him. I said to him that he would be a great young man. Nevertheless, he didn't really look like my older son. Although the scene was vivid, slowly I woke up. Session was 17 minutes long.

075-030512
NONPHYSICAL REALITY

The deep-rooted beliefs from the experience of the physical reality carry on to the afterlife. ———

After meditation, I went back to bed being conscious in keeping still. Before long, mild vibrations and out of body movements came. It took a while to complete the process. I was concerned about not having enough air to sustain the entire process. Afterwards, I was slightly out of breath but able to settle down.

While I was upside down, I asked to be taken to see my childhood friend. I felt a sudden change of scene and the whizzing of the surrounding.

In the next moment, I was bumping around in the bedroom. I felt restless and I got out of the room to the living room. I couldn't see much because I felt my eyes were shut closed due to dried mucus. I couldn't open them even with my hands. It was quite dark, and I was just feeling my way to the entryway. I was feeling the wall, the baseboard and the leg of a bench with my hands.

Moments after, my eyes opened and a vivid scene appeared right in front of me. While I was flying, I kicked out my left heel, flexed my left foot and straightened my left leg to give myself more power.

I had a vague false awakening before waking up at 7:25 am. Note: Throughout that day at work, I just felt like rotating, flexing and extending my two feet.

076-030912

THE NONPHYSICAL PAIN

---

*Only familiar past experiences could bring
about responses in my soul.*

After 45' of meditation, I went back to bed and slowly drifted into the transition state. I fixated my attention to five spots in space but only one at a time. Mild vibrations came before the out of body movements, which didn't follow through. But on the second time around, I simply just jumped out of my body.

Immediately, I felt someone grabbing me very hard from behind especially on my left arm pit. It was very uncomfortable. I tried to remove it with the reciting of the 9words Mantra but to no avail. So, I increased my strength and force in reciting the Mantra. Before long, the grip was loosened. I turned around and saw a girl. As I was approaching her, she signaled she had to leave. I drifted into unconscious dreams thereafter.

077-031512
WHO'S WATCHING

*My soul remains active with my body at rest
but not true conversely.*

After meditation, I went back to bed. As I was trying to be still, I heard my wife in the bedroom. (Note: She was already at work in real time). Without any vibration or out of body movement, I got out of my body. I floated supinely to the corner and from there I asked to stand upright. I also asked for clarity twice.

As I was walking around the bed, I would also look at the place where my physical body slept. I saw someone but not clearly under the blanket. However, I just knew full well that was me sleeping without any doubt. I walked out towards another room. My wife had the TV on. Then I watched a vivid scenery of nature in the rain. Following a false awakening in the bedroom, I slowly woke up. It all took 20 minutes.

078-040512
TIME VS INSTANT

Instant gratification is without the journey of the process.
However, experience of our lives defines our souls.

After meditation, I went back to bed. Out of nowhere, I found myself at an open place facing the open sky. I just started flying but I wasn't moving fast enough. Therefore, I attempted to visualize myself being at the destination.

I got to the peak of the mountain in a flash. Thereby, I realized that if you could visualize the final scene, you might be there instantaneously. On the contrary, if you visualized yourself getting there via whatever means, then you would be going through the process to get there.

After coming down from the peak, I was at a place where a beastly looking dog was leaning on me. Even though that made me a little uncomfortable, I kept my mind blank from any fear or emotion. I understood that when I was empty, the dog would also be empty and calm. Shortly, the dog's owner told me it's okay to go into an elevator together.

Before long, I was hopping and dancing, being in such a joy and bliss. I also floated up in the air watching many activities on the ground. There was a false awakening lasted for a while before I woke up. It was a 30-minute session.

HENRY C WONG

079-041512

MY TEACHER

Sound, light and images, transmit instantly
throughout the realm of the afterlife.

After meditation, I went back to bed where my wife was still sleeping. I took up my usual sleeping position. There was no vibration but the out of body movements came. I saw my leg rising out of me. Slowly I moved out of my body without any disruption from my wife.

Then I moved to the far-left corner of the room. As I was asking for clarity, my wife came over and shoved some wrinkled sheet over me. I kept asking for more clarity several times. It turned glaringly bright to such a degree that my wife was offended, turned away and disappeared.

After that, I attempted to go through the glass window to a beautiful scenery outside. I was stuck halfway through the glass, but I continued until I broke free. Once I was out, I just wanted to fly. I saw a lot of people, beings and scenes that I didn't recognize or remember. I flew around a bit. I was just very happy and filled with joy. I was singing and dancing. I vividly remembered my feelings at that time.

Suddenly, I thought of my Teacher. I started to recite the 9words Mantra while being mindful of Him.

I was facing an open space and a lot of stairs leading down to a village town. I went through more unfamiliar scenes before drifting into two false awakenings. Eventually I woke up. That was a long session of 45 minutes.

080-042012
HIGH FREQUENCY BLUE

The frequency of various colors might be an indication of different realms.

A fter an hour of meditation, I went back to bed. There was no vibration. I just jumped out of my body in the bedroom. Immediately after, I flew off following streams of blue color clouds. At the end of the streams, I got a glimpse of something not human before it quickly disappeared. At times, I also saw different exotic images in the streams. Not long afterwards, I woke up. It was a quick session of 10 minutes.

081-042312
LIVING ON MOON

The soul can be awakened even while still within the body.

After meditation, I went back to bed. Suddenly, a strange phenomenon happened. Even before the out of body phase initiated, I was already experiencing from the non-physical perspective. I, the nonphysical me, was feeling the subtle vibration firsthand while leaving slowly from the body. But the physical body couldn't sustain the absolute stillness. So, it all stopped. Then I tried again. The out of body movements came and I flew off immediately.

I flew all over the place just like a fighter jet pilot. I showed up in a gymnasium with lots of students. I wanted to do something unusual, such as stretching my leg up until my foot well above my head. I went out to the street. I pushed some lady away from some oncoming danger. As I flew straight up, she held on to me and I had to break away from her.

I got a feeling that I was about to wake up. So, I visualized the moon and being there, instead of asking to be taken to the moon. Without any lag, I saw the moon craters. I asked my wife who didn't look like her, to check out the moon. She felt the cold from a low leaky opening. I went over to another room to see my younger son who was in his tween. Then I got this feeling that I was about to wake up. As everything was fading away, I told myself to remember everything. I also envisioned coming straight back without any stopovers of false awakening. There was none this time. It was a 20-minute session.

082-042412

HOVERING MACHINE

The immaterial afterlife has recorded impressions of machines from the physical worlds.

After an hour of meditation and hard breathing practices, I went back to bed. Subtle signal and vibration came. I felt drifting a little above my body in the right direction. Again, I wasn't able to follow through and retreated back into my body. But I kept still and when the second time came, it was a lot stronger enabling me to complete the out of body process.

Immediately, I saw a large canopy looking machine hovering over me. The machine showed clear details on its intricate parts. I was touching them with my hands.

I switched from flying to walking into other rooms. I saw an object at the end of the room which looked like a small baby wrapped tightly after birth. I went over to unwrap it. It was a bottle of some kind even though I did hear crying beforehand. Then I drifted into unconscious dreams.

083-050412
FREE SPIRIT

---

*An inquisitive soul could manifest unexpected
image sequences.*

After an hour of meditation, I went back to bed a little before 7:00 am. I told myself to get up at 7:30 to go to work. There wasn't any out of body movement. When I became conscious, I told myself twice, "Take me to my Teacher."

Suddenly, I found my wife by the bathroom door pulling me towards her with some long strings. When I got to the door, I saw a 10-speed bike by the side. Immediately, I realized that I was in a dream, and I had this attitude of, "Let's go and play."

When I entered the bathroom, she complained of loud noises. People were using electric saw cutting through our ceiling from the upper floor. There was a small bike dangling through the opening. I crawled slowly through to the upper floor. I saw several male workers sawing and working on something. I was checking each one of them to identify who could be my Teacher.

There was a man who came towards me and sat down. I wasn't sure if he was my Teacher but his gait, face and physique were quite similar to my Teacher. I was wondering if we were ever neighbors before.

Then I went outside and had this tremendous energy to fly full throttle, aimlessly everywhere. I saw a few large planets in the scene. Moments later, I found myself indoor punching hard on the brick wall and not feeling any pain.

Shortly, I went outside again. As I flew away, I turned around and zoomed into the place where I took off. The scene became more and more clear. I was back on the roof of an old Chinese tile roof house. I was taking big leaps in the air on the roof and gripping onto those loose tiles. I also tried a triple-jump in the air to a distant building and made it. I said, "This's how it feels to leap and fly like those ancient martial artists."

I felt I had been out for a long time and got a sense that I should go back. I had a false awakening that fooled me. It showed me 9:45 and I was supposed to be late to work. I called the office saying I overslept. Whatever the receptionist was saying I couldn't really hear. Slowly I woke up again at 7:32. It all took only 35 minutes.

Note: I felt very good afterwards. My body was loosening up and all joints were not stiff. As I stretch, I had this soothing feeling throughout the body.

084-050512
TRANSDUCTION OF THOUGHTS

Transduction of messages is not limited within the physical realm.

During my hour meditation, I experienced sharp pain in my mid section stomach area. With breathing and light visualization practices, the pain went away. After meditation, I went back to bed.

At one point, I was focusing on some square dark objects in my mind. And simultaneously, I had the will and thought of leaving my body. Shortly after, I sensed movement and floating to the right within my body.

Then the scene became clear and vivid. I was floating in a supine position and clearly felt some force moving me over the bed back to the left. After that, I woke up and drifted back into dreams. It was about 60' long.

Note: it was not my active physical mind that thought of leaving the body. Instead, my awakened consciousness of my soul initiated since I had already unknowingly drifted into a transitional state.

085-051612
BORDERS BETWEEN REALMS

A glimpse of the future...

After an hour of meditation, I went back to bed. I was lying on my left side and easily attaining stillness. When I was about to effectuate the out of body process, I heard my wife coming into the room.

Nevertheless, I ignored her presence and proceeded quickly. Without any vibration, I just jumped out of my body swiftly and moved to the corner of the room. However, I had never seen that room before. Immediately after, I asked for clarity twice. The scene of the room came alive instantly. I also saw my wife at the other corner of the room by the twin bed.

Henceforth, I had not requested to go anywhere. I just pointed my two Dharma Hand Seals straight up in the open. Directly after, the scene changed and there wasn't any speeding inward or outward. I ended up in a nice high-rise apartment. I was with my younger son who was in his teen. When I looked out of the window, the world outside was very futuristic much like a picture right out of a sci-fi movie.

Moving to another scene, I was flying all over the place and doing flips in midair aimlessly. There was nothing that

I really wanted to do or see. Slowly, I woke up and simultaneously I still could feel myself being pulled back into my physical body.

086-060212
REALM OF TRANSFORMATIONS

Half of the time, my soul could seemingly change images in the afterlife.

After meditation, I went back to bed at 7:02 am. Apparently, I was awakened and alert. Even amid this alertness, a subtle signal and vibration came. Thereby, I floated out of my body and going all over the room.

Soon after, I was back in bed thinking that I had just woke up. I knew I was in a false awakening when my head was at the foot of the bed instead.

Next, I felt something on my right moving up and down. There was a thing in white right in front of me. It didn't resemble anything. I got up and directed both of my Dharma Seals at it, hoping to deliver it. It didn't really work, and this thing was gnawing on my hands.

An instant later, I saw a human body lying in bed in a fetal position. I was trying to visualize it being transformed into emptiness. That body slowly flattened out and disappeared. After that, I toggled back and forth between unconsciousness and awakening state. Session turned out to be 40 minutes long.

087-060312
GIRLS' VOICES

You can hear only resonating voices to your distinct vibrational signature.

After meditation, I went back to bed. When I sensed my out of body phase was about to fail, I tried to visualize myself going over to the other side. It worked.

I was floating around a little bit. I was flying closed to the ground where there were many large pits on the ground with debris and rocks around them. Inside the pits, there were creatures unknown to me. They looked like crabs or lobsters. I heard girls' voices telling me something about them. When I couldn't hover high enough, my feet were dragging across the ground. I could vividly feel the small gravels.

Next off, I was at a place with a lot of people around. As usual, I was bored and restless. I saw someone burning something with a lighter. I went over and grabbed it to burn the middle of my right palm. I just wondered if it would be painful. And could I be burned? I couldn't sense any pain over the flame or see any burn marks on my palm.

In another scene, I saw large glass windows on the second floor of a building. I wanted to see if I could go through the glass. But there was this person nearby kept interrupting me. Despite being only halfway through the glass, I had to withdraw due to the interference.

Thereafter, I went flying again. I was debating if I should visit any planets. When I looked up, the sky was filled with burning spaceships and other objects, but not stars or planets. I also heard voices from girls in many of those small flying spacecrafts. This was quite a long session of 65 minutes.

088-060412
ETERNAL SEEING

The soul sees much more and better than our eyes.

After an hour of meditation, I went back to bed. During the meditation, I was energized with an erected back. There was no obvious out of body movement. I was lying on my left side being very alert. I knowingly kept still and thought about leaving the body. What followed was simply to wait for it to happen.

From one moment of being alert in bed to the next moment of being in a totally different state, there was zero gap of time and space. The change was seamless and instantaneous.

Out of nowhere, I found myself lying down in a room not known to me. I was looking at a robotic creature with many mechanical extensions, each attached with either pincher or clamp. I asked for clarity three times to clear up the scene.

Then I stood up and hovered, dashing through another room out of the house. I went so fast that I had to tell myself to slow down. When I was out, my eyes felt clamped shut. I was peeping through a small opening from where I could see some landscapes in vivid details. I couldn't open my eyes wider with my hands. At that moment, it reminded me what my Teacher said in class yesterday, "Our eyes are actually shut." Session was 30' long.

089-060712
FOLLOW THE DRAGON

━━━━━━━━━

The afterlife would continuously reveal to you.

After meditation, I went back to bed. At first, I was just being passive, and my mind just wandered slowly into an unconscious dream state. But later, I snapped out of that and concentrated on being still.

Quickly, the signal came, and I started floating out of my body. During the process, I had few moments of disturbance from the feeling of drooling at the left corner of my mouth. Nevertheless, I maintained my momentum and chose to just ignore my drooling.

Once I was stabilized, I asked for clarity twice and opened my eyes wide open. It really felt like my eyes were open wide. I heard loud noises. Soon after, I was being pulled by a big, long rod in front of me. It was pulling me all over the room and the house. In a flash, it changed to a purple crystal rod with rough jagged surface. For a moment, I was a little startled, but I decided to just follow it.

It was going fast out of the house and then into space. I was reciting the 9words Mantra here and there. The rod later changed into something animated. The changes were continuous and transient. Slowly, it took on the shape of a dragon. In one moment, the dragon just broke up into countless small black pieces. I was looking on from the left-hand side. The dragon never stayed in one shape for very long.

Eventually, it changed into a short bulky creature which I had never seen before. It was marching forward on a mirror like ground surface with its own reflection. When we reached a stone arch opening, where many birdlike creatures gathered, the dragon was gone.

The scene changed and I was in a large room with people working. I asked one of them where was this place. I was even aware that I asked this question all the time. I went outside and saw tall buildings. I asked a policeman the same question and he said, "Rexford, London, England." I looked around and he got busy with someone else. I felt my eyes tired from opening wide. Everything settled down and I woke up. Session seemed long but only 15 minutes.

090-060912
KALEIDOSCOPIC EXPERIENCE

The fleeting impermanence seems especially pronounced in the afterlife.

After meditation, I went back to bed and my wife was sound asleep. She was breathing so hard that I couldn't settle down. Then I turned over to the left side and put an ear plug in my right ear. That helped me to be calm enough to carry on with my routine.

I was fixating my concentration in my mind rather than the body. Subsequently, the vibrations came like waves sweeping through my mind. I didn't just wait for it to happen as I did in the past. It happened on my third attempt of focusing on my mind. Swiftly I stood up and moved out of my body, hovering and floating to the end of the room. However, looking back at my bed, I didn't see my body.

Out of nowhere, I also experienced another separate out of body phase. I felt I literally floated off the bed together with my physical body and blanket, without separation. The feeling was so believable that I worried falling off the bed onto the floor.

I asked for crystal clarity twice and the room became vividly clear slowly from one small area to the entire room. It was so real that I felt like I was awakened in the physical world. I even worried that my wife might wake up to see me floating off the bed.

I looked out of the window and I saw a huge metal chain attached to my room, like a ship's anchor. I danced in front of a mirror in the room, but I couldn't see any reflection in the mirror.

I also saw high rise apartments all around me. Lots of those other windows had large dark purple flowers. As I panned across the area, I heard sound of chopping board as in Chinese cooking and people talking.

As I settled down, I also slowly drifted out of the scene and woke up without any false awakening. About 2 seconds after I woke up, my wife extended her arm over to touch me. That was perfect coordinated timing.

091-061212
IT HAPPENED TWICE

Body and soul fuse together so well, and yet can be separated in a flash.

After meditation, I went back to bed. Once my focus was fixated on my mind, signal and vibration would sweep across my head region. On the second sweep, I followed that sweeping momentum and ended up over the right side of the bed.

Before I stood up, I went through a detailed out of body process. At first, I was flat on my back. My legs rose up first with my back still touching, followed by whole body levitation and floating out.

When I made a turn hitting the wall with my feet, the sensation of the contact with the wall felt real. The scene of the room was getting so realistic that I could have mistaken it as the real thing.

While I was hovering on the right side of the bed, I saw 3 young girls in their early teens. They were my sister and nieces or cousins but I couldn't see their faces. And at that moment, I woke up.

I kept still and my focus on my mind. Quickly, I left the body the second time. I was floating in a prone position and rotating horizontally for a while. When it stopped, I stood up and went to my study room. Before the glass door, I was curious to see if the front courtyard was the same. I peeped through the curtains, and it looked like my current physical front yard. The square planter was still there though not defined.

As I walked out of my study room, I saw someone got out of the bedroom with a blanket covering head to toe. I didn't want to bother with it and walked away quickly. I woke up afterwards. It was a session of 30 minutes.

092-061312
MARVELOUS EXPLORATIONS

The afterlife is like a two-way mirror which can see us in the physical world, but we're oblivious to its existence.

After an hour of meditation and breathing practices, I went back to bed lying on my left side. I drifted into a state of unconscious dream at first. When I woke up. I still had the last image of being in a room with a woman and a child whom I didn't recognize. At the same moment, I remembered to concentrate in my head and wait for the out of body movements.

Shortly, a subtle sweeping vibration came. At first, I turned to the right to be flat on my back. My legs floated over to the right. Seamlessly, I shifted right into the scene of the above-mentioned last image.

While I was drifting standing up in another room, everything seemed so real. I could remember vivid details of things around the room but forgot quickly afterwards. I had no reference in the physical world to compare to, or because I just didn't know what they were, or they were just mundane items.

As I looked out a small window, I saw a jungle of trees. When I looked closely, I saw many leopards scattered all over the place. Shortly after, they became anaconda heads and other animals. I was concerned they might be able to break the window. As soon as I became slightly fearful, bad thoughts immediately came up. Right away I transformed those thoughts into emptiness and reciting the 9words Mantra.

I ran swiftly out of the room into an open space. The scene became a little blurry yet stable. I asked for clarity couple times and took off my sunglasses. Things became vivid again.

By then, I was just very anxious to do something, to test something or to explore the scene. I held up a pair of glasses with a plastic frame. I bent the arm of the frame. It flexed but didn't break.

Right afterwards, I opened my hands and looked at my palm prints. The line from my wrist to the middle finger in my physical body was interrupted by a 4 points star. I saw that line in dark red, a thick line with that same interrupting section missing. I also saw red lines and red patches on both palms. They did look like real hands, not like the dark smoke in my previous experience. Shortly, I just woke up from this 20-minute session.

093-061512

MEETING MY OTHER FAMILY

My soul has all my timeless secrets.

After meditation, I went back to bed lying on my left side. When I experienced the vibrations, I was a little out of breath. I didn't really want to move and break the stillness. I turned over to the right a little to lessen the pressure on my heart.

During that time, I heard people and noises but I just ignored them. Out of body movements came and I flipped to the right. Next moment, I was floating supinely all over the room. I was looking at my legs and feet while they were touching things, until I went back to bed with my face on the pillow.

Before long, I was in another scene where I saw supposedly my son, not my current two sons, handling some dead pets in a tank with another woman. I was mad and yelling at that woman, my wife apparently but not looking like my current wife. She was not happy either. Afterwards, I calmed down and realized that I rarely ever got mad in out of body experience.

In another scene of multitude of people, I flew up hovering over them. As I flew over other places, I saw people going about their businesses and tanks, machine, vehicles, etc. I had this realization that these countless living beings and activities filled the universe. They were the existence and the "One". I woke up shortly after. Session was 20 minutes long.

094-061812
STRANGE REALMS

Reincarnation might be a better choice than wandering in the afterlife.

After an hour of meditation, I went back to bed and assumed the same sleeping position. My breathing was slightly heavy today. All I did was thinking of what I would want to do.

After the focus on my third eye brought about couple quick subtle vibrations, I swiftly ended up on the floor at the foot of my bed. While I was crossing over, my slight laboring breathing made me feel that I might not be able to maintain the out of body process. I got up from the floor trying to break away from something like a bed sheet that enclosed me. In one instant, I thought it could be made disappeared.

After I broke free, I immediately asked to be taken to the moon. I did also think of being there instead of going there. It didn't happen either way. So, I went over to the windows on the left. I thought by looking outside, I could tell if I was dreaming. When I looked over to the side of the window, there was an old fashion dialing telephone on the table. At once, I knew it was a dream.

I wanted to test something. I opened the window, leaned out and saw a whole lot of people outside of the window.

Apparently, I was on the ground floor. I said, "Hey!" They all stopped walking and froze up. I heard someone saying that I shouldn't be doing that. I just always liked to do things to confirm the realism of my surrounding.

After that, I ran down the street with a razor blade in my hand and finding a place for it. There were stores on the right of the street. I felt without any clothes on. Glad to wake up directly just in time. The session was 20 minutes long.

095-062112
ELUSIVENESS OF TIME

Some journeys are just unremarkable and puzzling.

I got up late at 7:00 this morning. After 60' of meditation, I went back to bed. It was already after 8:00. With focus in my mind and couple subtle signals, out of body movements came. I was bouncing around the room like a steel ball in a pinball machine. I called for clarity twice and it got clearer.

Then I saw a dark blue crumpled up bed sheet moving in the air and approaching me. I got restless. So, I spun around to change the scene.

Moment later, I showed up in another room. On the table in front of the window, there was something resembling a cellphone. But the date and time were blackened out. I also saw a contraption which reminded me of something in the past. I was thinking I must have time traveled to the past. I woke up thereafter.

096-062312
REPENTANCE PRAYER

There's something I can take with me to the afterlife.

After 40' of meditation, feeling tired and I went back to bed. After settling in for a while on the left, couple subtle signals came before a strong one swept over me.

I found myself rotating around my head with my feet over my left nightstand. Subsequently, I floated slowly out of the bedroom through the door. When I reached the curtains, I reached out to find an opening. Finally, I drew the curtains and looked outside. It was breathtaking, a vast scene with blurry scenery of the outdoor, river and cliffs.

I asked for more clarity twice. It started with a small window opening in the middle of the field of vision. The small patch of clarity gradually expanded more and more with vivid clarity of rivers and ocean, running between stunning sheer cliffs and mountain range. Black color cliffs and ocean water kept changing in their formations.

Shifting to the next scene, I was in a crowded place with lots of people walking around. Suddenly, I remembered right before going back to bed in the physical reality, that I set out to do "Golden Light Between Palms" practice in the afterlife.

I just stopped there and carried out the practice in front of a girl who was wearing a heavy jacket.

During the whole practice, I simultaneously recited clearly a long Repentance Prayer in its entirety. But I mistook a yellow patch in the back of her jacket as the golden light when my hands stopped.

Afterwards, I walked around a bit and intended to fly. But I felt a some small being or a small kid gabbing my legs. So, I couldn't fly off and I struggled to fight him off. I even bit the fingers of a little hand. woke up thereafter. Session was 15 minutes long.

097-070712
ONE AND ONLY REALITY

_____

Countless unique one and only realities exist in each being.

After meditation, I went back to bed lying on my left. My wife was also there. As usual, I started out moving to the right and quickly back to the left, rolling off my bed slowly to the floor.

This was the first time I felt undeniably as one with my actual physical body. The sensation of rolling off the bed, touching the floor and my head touching the closet door further validated that belief. I was so sure without a shadow of a doubt.

What followed was me being on the floor experiencing a full body vibrational shock, and subsequent levitation off the floor. I floated supinely towards my study room. A moment later, I rose up and came back down in a prone position at the bedroom door in the hallway. My wife walked out and bumped my head, as if I was invisible.

Suddenly, I was curious if my physical body was still sleeping in bed. When I saw another person whom I didn't recognize in bed, I was puzzled. I was also curious at the time about how I would look like. I went into my wife's bathroom and looked at the mirror. I saw myself. Although not too clear, but I knew it was me.

Then I went to get in bed with that other guy who was supposed to be me. I tried to merge with him back into one body. We talked a little and decided that was not going to work. I just had to live with it.

I went out to the living room. There were a bunch of people, including my wife who was a Filipino I didn't recognize. I questioned her who the other guy was. She mentioned a mutual friend named Nelson. The other guy also looked Filipino.

At that moment, I felt liberated because I had a reason to leave all of them and live my own life. This time I felt everything was so real. There wasn't the slightest doubt that it was the reality, and there were no thoughts about any other place that I needed to go back to. Slowly, everything faded away and I woke up. It was a 20-minute session.

Note: I don't have any Filipino friends or knowing anyone by the name Nelson.

098-071812
THE BIG BANG

Whatever my soul decided in the afterlife, might be completely beyond the expectation of my body.

After two hours of meditation, I went back to bed. There's no way of telling whether an out of body session or merely just a lucid dream would develop from a half awaken transitional state. All I could do was preparing myself and wait.

There were no vibrations or out of body movements. In a flash, I showed up in a room. I asked to be taken to the ocean. Suddenly, I was floating and submerging in water. There was debris floating all around me.

Then I put both of my Dharma Seals together. And I asked to be taken to the beginning of the universe, the Big Bang. I did worry a bit about getting harmed, but nothing happened. I woke up thereafter. Short session of 10 minutes.

099-072512
SENSATION VS IMAGE

*The sensation connecting with the image
constitutes their causation.*

After an hour of meditation, I went back to bed. The sensation of entire body switched into another different state. Right after a quick roll to the right, I floated right out of my body. As I was hovering, floating and flipping around the room, I asked for clarity quietly in my mind couple times. The scene became vivid and clear.

I wanted to go somewhere else, and I mumbled about taking me somewhere. I put my hands together and pointed straight up and closed my eyes. Despite the sensation of rushing through the air, I remained in the room when I opened my eyes. Apparently, it didn't work.

Then I moved on to open my bedroom door and looked out to the family room. I was startled to see two 10 speed bikes in the family room because there shouldn't be any. When I walked out to the living room, there were bikes everywhere.

I drew the curtains and looked out to the front courtyard, but the center square planter was missing. There were hedges instead of fences and irregular flagstones all over the grass. I heard kids playing ball out there. The dining room area opened to a small lake.

A while later, I woke up to a false awakening where my brother in his tween and my sister were right next to me. They were bumping into me causing me out of my meditative state. I was angry because I couldn't continue with my practice. I yelled at them and chased them away. Without a break, my sister started blow drying her hair right next to me. I told her just how inconsiderate of her. I woke up afterwards. It all took 25 minutes.

100-081512
LOVE AND ATTACHMENT

Transcending all the stored creation...nothingness remains.

After meditation, I went back to bed being very alert. Without any signal, I lightly just flipped to the right side and back, rotating within the body. Next off, I found myself standing at the bedroom door. I proceeded to open it and walked out to the living room. Shortly, I levitated in a supine position, hovering and floating all over. I also inhaled continuously to move up even higher.

I was very much aware that I was in another realm, because I felt I could easily withdraw back into to my body. This feeling was constant throughout the whole time. I went out in the rain and came back in. I tried to make a call on a touch phone.

Quite unexpectedly, I found my younger son in his tween who still looked the same. He didn't say anything. I hugged him and said, "I always love you." I cried and wiped my eyes. He was puzzled as to why I was so emotional. I had this feeling that he also existed in the physical world. The sobbing slowly woke me up. The session was 25 minutes long. When I told my wife in the morning, I was still all choked up.

101-082412

NUMBER 3245

*Sequential continuum of images creates the
perception of time in the observer.*

After meditation, I went back to bed and my wife was also
there. I got into my usual sleeping position on my left side.
I felt the signal. I went ahead with the out of body movements, even though my wife might interrupt me at any time.

I felt myself pulling away from my body, but I couldn't see
anything. So, I asked for clarity. It all became more visible but
still quite dark. I wanted to float out of the room right away
but to no avail.

Afterwards, I was fixating at an image of a small pebble
on the floor. At the same time, I had this feeling that I was
about to wake up. Instead, I saw colorful designs for children
on the walls in a hallway. I said to myself that I had seen them
before. I was happy, singing and dancing, walking into another room. There were people and children.

I looked across noticing a store with those large calendars on display. I went over and started looking for the year.
I saw 3245 roughly. In my mind, I said, "That's about a thousand years ahead in the future." I couldn't remember much
after that. It was a session of 30 minutes.

Note: I have been using an email address with the four numbers 2534 since the year 2004. In the year of 2016, surprisingly the last 4 numbers of my new passport also turned out to be 2534.

102-082712
A DAY AT THE BEACH

There's no way to tell, if my experience in the physical world is merely a replay of my past occurrence. Thus, make every single lifetime worth living.

After meditation, I went back to bed lying on my left side. I told myself I needed to get up at 7:30 am. Before long, I found myself flying and hovering over a vividly beautiful seashore beach, bright and colorful.

Slowly, I lost altitude and walked about instead. I said to myself that it was very realistic. I even reached out to touch someone walking by. The feeling of the touch was lifelike. I was happy and excited. I lay down on my back facing the sky with my two arms extended upwards and palms out. I looked up and showed my gratitude for this amazing scene.

There were very high and large dune-like structures with vertical recessed channels running over them. In the middle of several of these dunes, there were taller transmission type towers jutting out to the sky.

There were also numerous people all facing out to the water. I walked over seeing people throwing rocks at those big fishlike creatures, apparently stranded in the shallow water. Thereafter, it was uneventful and slowly I woke up. The clock showed 7:30 exactly.

103-082812
MY SEASHORE HOUSE

Strong, meaningful relationships derive energy from mutual spiritual bondings.

After meditation, I went back to bed at 7:48 am lying on my left side. I just froze up and gazed at any plain image in my mind. Immediately, I felt the pulling from my right and instantly I was out of the body.

It was very dark, and I couldn't see a thing. As I was moving around the bed to the bedroom door, I asked for clarity several times and it slowly got better. When I reached my study room at the glass door, I asked to be outside but to no avail.

I continued to walk to other parts of the house. I found my younger son in his tween. I thought my older son was also there but didn't get to see him. I talked to him a bit and commented on how run down the house looked.

I walked out of the house and realized that the house was situated at the seashore. I saw many Pelicans resting at the pier. I yelled out, "I saw this just the other day in my dream." I was very excited. I forgot what came after until I just wanted to fly. I decided to take my younger son with me. We both went straight up to a certain point and just came back down. After a false awakening, I woke up at 8:05.

104-083012
TELEKINESIS

Different abilities exist in different realms.

After meditation, I went back to bed lying on my left side. Quickly after, I drifted to the right. Right at that moment, I felt my wife walking to the edge of the bed talking to me. I was wondering why she was not at work already. I didn't want to get bothered and continued floating off.

Shortly, I found myself sitting in a small room. There was a big portable machine, the size of an upright refrigerator. I was using my will power and slowly waving my hand up to move the upper portion of the machine upward. And then I had it push against the wall. I also waved my hand to move the entire machine to the left. I said to myself, "I should be able to do this to change bad situations in my dreams." After that I went out to another room where somebody was doing some work. Just random dreams before I woke up much later.

105-083112

THE EVER-CHANGING UNIVERSE

Life is in flux...so is the afterlife.

After meditation, I went back to bed lying on my left. My wife was already up and about. Then it just happened. This time, I could see clearly my arms and legs rolling to the right, along with my body floating off to the foot of the bed. From there, I continued floating feet first towards my study room. When my feet reached the upper left corner of the room, I had this feeling that this time I would be going somewhere else on the outside.

As soon as my feet pushed through the glass door, I saw the expanse of the universe, a multitude of sparkling little stars in clusters, trails and strands formations. They constantly formed, changed and disappeared. I couldn't recognize any of them, just marveled at the majestic display. When I saw a long trail of spots, I wondered if it were a dragon. After a while, I was back in my bed, complaining about my wife touching me and startled me.

Nevertheless, that was merely a false awakening.

HENRY C WONG

106-091212
SPECTACULAR WONDERS

My soul seems to be able to control the scenes...

After an hour of meditation, I went back to bed. There wasn't any signal or out of body movement at first. Suddenly, I ended up in a very spectacular scene with vivid colors and landscapes. The scenery was full of life, emitting overwhelming noises and displaying volatile phenomena of nature. I was not afraid. On the contrary, I was ecstatic and pleased to see all that in front of me. The scene was both expansive and explosive.

Meanwhile, I did something strange by swiping my hand across and downward with palm facing down. The scene immediately settled down and became quiet. I thought if I could do that, I must be able to bring myself to fly. Sadly, that didn't work.

And I didn't know how long afterwards before I became awakened in the transition state with the subtle signal. Right away, I started drifting to the right. I was getting very comfortable with the whole process. I was even thinking of what to do during this process of leaving my body. Apparently, these thoughts interrupted the process, causing me to drift back into the body and facing down. From that position, I continued drifting up and backwards.

I felt I was holding my breath since this out of body phase started. I was also thinking that my breathing practices must have helped me to hold my breath without the need to breathe. The process was taking a little longer than usual. Eventually, I recoiled back into the body. The whole session was about 45' long.

107-091512
PARTY CRASHER

_____

The sun also shines in the spiritual realm. _____

I woke up with a moderate stomachache. After 60' of meditation and breathing exercise, pain was gone and I went back
to bed. Today, I was a little edgy and that might interfere with
the out of body process. In other words, I was not 100% at
ease or totally surrendering to the process.

Nevertheless, as soon as I was able to reach those states,
the out of body movements proceeded smoothly. During the
process, I told myself that it would be alright to breathe and
not holding my breath before crossing over.

After couple failed attempts, at the third time my out of
body movements made it across. Without a break, I found
myself already in a totally unfamiliar scene. I asked for clarity
and the scene cleared up. I did some flying and hovering
before walking a seemingly familiar place with people talking
loudly. I also walked to a place where the sun was so bright
that I couldn't see anything. Couple clarity requests cleared
up somewhat. I had to open my eyes that were seemingly
stuck shut with dried mucus.

In the next scene, I saw people having a boating contest.
While the person who was in charge talking to everyone, I

went out to the water from shore to feel the water. I felt it but couldn't sense its wetness. He stopped talking and everybody suddenly directed all the attention to me. I attempted to fly away but I couldn't fly fast enough or high enough. They were shooting some projectiles at me.

I finally got trapped in a small closet. I turned around to fight with him. I twisted his arm back and injected his arm with his syringe. He turned into a young woman and there was also a very young guy next to her. When the scene became dull, I just had this feeling that I was about to wake up. There was no false awakening before I woke up from this 30-minute session.

108-092912
BUDDHA IN CHINESE CHARACTER

My soul was being tested...

During the meditation, I got restless. After less than 60' of meditation, I went back to bed at 7:00. My wife came in at the same time but it didn't matter to me.

I got settled in and dreamt a little. Then I focused on a patch of unidentifiable patterns in my third eye area. Signal came and quickly I just rolled to the right over my wife. I could even feel the contact with her body.

Immediately after, I was in a room full of people. It was quite clear, bright and vivid, but I still asked for more clarity. I realized I stumbled over words at times. I reached out to shake hands with a kid. I also hugged him just to see if I could feel the sensation of touch. I felt it but not as strong.

Then I went out to the open looking up the sky and I flew up. There were images of patterns up in the sky. I couldn't go too far or too high. Slowly, I descended back down on top of palm like brushes, which was holding me up.

Shortly after, I showed up in a room, sitting down and facing a blank wall. I said "Fo", which means Buddha. Then a single nonexistent Chinese character "女弗" was covering the wall. I said to myself that it was not correct. Nevertheless, right after I recited the 9words Mantra, the character on the wall changed to the correct form "佛". I didn't exactly recite it word by word, but I knew I did it. I also recited the entire Repentance Prayer as quickly as a thought.

Meanwhile, some people walked in. One of them was my sister. Slowly, I knew I was waking up. I even tried to do a spin to keep it longer. But it was too late. I woke up at 7:29 with no false awakening. Session was 30 minutes long.

109-100212
THIRD PERSON PERSPECTIVE

*My soul could also incarnate into an
unbodied consciousness.*

After 60 minutes of meditation, I went back to bed lying on my left. This time, I didn't roll to the right as usual. I just stood up and out of my body, hovering over the head area of my sleeping body.

Unexpectedly, I found out that I was looking from a perspective of a third person point of view, slightly behind my nonphysical body entity. I could see the entire body of the entity. With the control of my right hand, I was guiding my entity up high and around the room at will.

Gradually, my perspective drifted back to my body entity, which became myself once again. I directed myself up high right through the wall. I saw the universe full of specks of lights. I flew lightning fast through space, feeling the stars passing me by. But the space has no end to it. I wasn't going anywhere. I saw images of different patterns of the universe, where stars were no longer random. I saw the invisible patterns from the arrangement of the stars.

Slowly, I descended back to the ground. There were people around me. I was just sitting there on the ground. I attempted to touch a person who avoided me. Slowly I got this feeling that I was going back. There was no false awakening before I woke up thereafter. Session was 30 minutes long.

Note: During the day, I tried something by focusing at my third eye area. The subtle signal followed, analogous to an on/off switch.

110-100412
A FAMILIAR STRANGER

<hr>

Relationships are all fleeting moments.

After meditation, I went back to bed. This time, I rolled to the left and out of the body in a flash. I saw clearly a room not looking like my real bedroom, which used to be dim and dark. It looked very much like another place. I also asked for clarity to brighten it up even more.

Later, I moved to the front door and went outside. Supposedly, the sun was so bright that everything was whited out. I couldn't see a thing. Shortly after, I showed up at a place where I met up with a young man. I didn't recognize him, but he looked familiar. We talked and walked together, seemingly very close. When we reached a place under the open sky, I started levitating and hovering while he was looking on. Slowly, I woke up from this 20-minute session.

111-100812
NOTHING ISN'T ALIVE

The afterlife is no less lively than the physical world.

After meditation, I went back to bed lying on my left. Lately, there was no signal, no vibration and no need to focus on the mind. Even when I was fully awake and aware, instantly, I could be out of my body.

Suddenly, I saw my feet lifted above my head and my whole body followed. Then I turned, flipped, rotated and hovered until I rested on the floor. I saw an 8-12 inches tall toy like figure on the floor talking to me. I didn't know why I just shoved it across the room out to another room. From there, I found a lot more dolls, figures and robots, all seemed to be saying something to me or taunting me. I entered the room and they all vanished, replaced by plenty of people and kids. During the whole time, everything was very real and vivid. My eyes were wide open.

Once again, I was checking out the calendar. The first thing I was looking for was the year. I thought I won't be finding anything as in the past. This time however, I found the Year 980. I was expecting something in the 3-4 thousand years range. The year of 980 was from the past ancient time. There shouldn't be any modern day's technology. I looked out of the window and down, I saw ocean water turning into a large swimming pool. I was obviously in a high-rise apartment.

Back in the apartment, I took a lighter away from a person and tested the flame on my hand. I thought it shouldn't hurt because I did it before. But this time it hurt. Next, I pulled few strands of my hair and tested over the flame. They indeed extinguished. Suddenly, I gazed at the corner, and I knew it's over, I'm going back. I woke up at 7:11. It was a 19-minute-long session.

112-101812
INSTANT ARRIVALS

Despite the zero distance to all destinations in the afterlife...
Reaching them is an entirely different matter.

After meditation, I was tired and went back to bed lying on my left side at around 6:40 am. Initially, I had some hesitation leaving my body. In no time, I was already away somewhere else from my room. The scene was vividly real. However, I still asked for clarity couple times.

Afterwards, I just took off flying and said to myself, "Am I supposed to visualize being somewhere already instead of going through the passage?" I was thinking of the Eiffel Tower. Instantly, I showed up at a place where a whole lot of colored people around me. I asked them where's this place. They told me it's Paris. A moment later, I picked another destination, South Pole. I showed up at a place where numerous Japanese men gathered.

Shortly after, I woke up and drifted back into regular sleep till 9:00. There were other details that I couldn't remember, because I wrote this at the end of the day.

HENRY C WONG

113-102212
POSITIVE THOUGHTS

The afterlife can be quite responsive to my thoughts.

Today was the first day of 2 hours long meditation. I did a lot of breathing exercise to keep my neck and upper back straight. After meditation, I got quite tired, and I went back to bed lying on my left side.

With no signal, I just came right out of my body, floating supinely all over the bedroom. It was quite vivid and clear. I was staring at my feet the whole time. At times, I was vertically upside down.

When I reached the glass door, my feet went through with no problem. It felt like someone was guiding me. As I was going through the glass, the word "Stuck" appeared in my mind. Right away, my head and face couldn't go through and stuck there for a while. With a little struggle and pulling on the plastic like glass away from my face, I moved on to the next scene.

I was feeling my feet walking on large rocks. I saw again those animated cartoon characters. There was a funny looking duck with a very large beak and I touched it. Suddenly, I was looking down from a very high place and felt the weakness in my legs. I also had a guy holding a small gun pointing at me. I took it from him and pointed it back at him. It turned into a lighter. I woke up thereafter. It was a session of 30 minute.

114-102312
IMAGES OF REALITY

The crossover is an overlapping superimposed border between realms.

During the 2 hours of meditation, my neck and upper back were tired and not straight. I also had pain in my left index finger due to occupational stress. Afterwards, I went back to bed lying on my left side.

Initially, I drifted into a short dream before being awakened. I kept still and attempted to trigger the out of body movements. Nevertheless, it worked better if I hadn't imposed my will onto the process. So, I just kept still and let it come.

Shortly after, I rolled to the right about halfway, quickly rolled back to the left and quickly out of the body. Immediately, I was in an unfamiliar room, small but cozy and vividly real. There was no need to ask for clarity. I just floated slowly all over the room, from hovering to walking on the carpet floor. There was also a chandelier. I drew the curtains and saw a wall of green hedges right outside of the glass door.

Before long, I felt I was about to wake up. I always just fixated on one image as I woke up. The transition to the awakening state was very interesting. The fixed image of the room occupied the entire rectangular space which we normally see with our eyes closed. As I was waking up, that image remained intact and vivid. I was even wondering if my physical eyes had already been open. It was very lifelike. At one point, I realized my physical eyes were still shut and that last image could have been mistaken as a physical reality because I was already awakened. The session was 15 minutes long.

115-102712

SPIN LIKE AN ATOM

When an image freezes up, perspective switches between body and soul.

During the 2 hours of meditation, I struggled to keep my neck and back straight throughout. I was tired and went back to bed lying on my left side. My wife was also in bed. Though it was cold, it didn't take long. When the image in my mind just froze up, I felt myself leaving the body. I went out a little and came back inside of the body. I maintained the state of stasis and the out of body movements started again. This time, I came out of the body and ended up in a room that was unfamiliar to me. I was still in bed with a large blanket around me.

Out of nowhere, I saw a yellow highlighter in front of my face while I was lying on my stomach in a prone position. The highlighter was spinning and traveled towards my face. I didn't flinch and I was not frightened. I trusted it would not hit me or hurt me. It did just that four more times with gradually faster spherical spinning and hurtled to just shy of my face.

In between its hurtling towards me, it went off to the side. After the last one, it was just spinning in front of me radiating off a colorful outer rim which gradually became larger. At the same time, its background behind and around emerged as a vivid and clear image.

In the next scene, I just knew this place was a poor part of Hawaii. There were people that I didn't know around a housing project. I also saw an old Victorian European ship flotilla in the harbor. I went out to a muddy and run down place. There were couple sleazy characters at the side of the alley. I wanted to get out of that scene. I sat inside of a very small tent like enclosure expecting to wake up in another scene. Shortly, I showed up at a Chinese place where people eating and talking, nothing special. Afterwards, I woke up from this 30-minute session.

116-102812
BUSY TRAVELING

─────────

My soul has always been a traveler.　─────────

After two hours of meditation, I went back to bed lying on my left. My wife was still in bed. At one time, I had already formed an image in my mind, but it froze up due to the noise from my wife's movements.

Nevertheless, I continued, and image formed again. As I was focusing on it and its details, the image started moving and evolving. They were just some inanimate parts and objects. I told myself I should start paying more attention to the details, so that I could recount them later. Whenever I moved too fast by just glancing over the image, it won't hold up and continue. It simply just vanished.

Before long, I showed up walking down a street with stores in a non-Asian city. Again, I wanted to pay attention to the details of the stores on my right. I came across a store with a lot of people talking inside. I walked in through a long corridor and there were parrots talking. I walked out and wondered what city it was.

Shifting to the next scene, I was in the backseat of a small car with another man whom I apparently knew. They let me out in an open place with mud on unpaved ground. I was supposed to meet him later.

While I was walking, I thought of my wife back home where I came from. At that time, I was aware of my existence in both places. I also told myself not to think of my wife or my body, because it would pull me back home and ending this scene.

As I was about to leave the fading scene, I attempted to do a spin to switch to another scene instead of waking up. I ended up in another open area. I was able to fly low right above a city with high-rises, like Manhattan. I did have a glimpse of myself flying over it.

Shortly, I ended at a table with three others. A woman accused another of associating with a gang. I found the company not too friendly. So, I left. Next moment, I showed up in a dark room with many medical equipments. Couple people left me in there alone. I was in bed knocking over something and suspecting myself having cancer. I woke up thereafter. Session was 30 minutes long.

117-103012
FREE FALL

Fears and beliefs perpetuate in my soul.

After meditation, I went back to bed lying on my left side. I tried to stay awake even with my eyes slightly open. No memory of dreaming before I realized I was driving a large bus. I couldn't really stop the bus at the intersection. It just wanted to take off.

A policeman on one of those two wheels scooter got in front and I hit him off to the side. When the bus started to climb an almost vertical slope, I had to really step on it. We kept driving up to the top which was a small patch of land. Beyond that spot was this open expanse above the abyss, with dark clouds and white light below.

It happened so fast that the bus immediately started falling, along with myself. Usually, I would just bail out and wake up because I didn't want to face that unthinkable final moment. At that instant, I decided to stay with it and just let the fall to take me.

After a while of that straight down free fall, I slowed down and floated. I was traveling all over through an undefined space with undefined images of clouds, colors and lights. Besides, nothing was recognizable. As I reached a more confined space with undefined patterns, I felt my physical body back home needed to cough. I coughed very slightly and the scene in front of me stopped moving and froze up, slowly faded out before I woke up. The session was 15 minutes long.

118-110312
CHANGE SCENE

━━━━━━━━━━

━━━━
My soul didn't seem to know what scenes would come next.
━━━━

After two hours of meditation, I went back to bed at 7:05. My wife was still in bed. This time, I was not trying to be alert for the whole process. Few random thoughts came up and I shifted to the no-mind state. Signals followed but I didn't know when I crossed over to the other side.

I found myself driving behind an old car which was speeding up on a large area of grass. I also drove very fast and caught up with him. By then, I was running into a lot of trees and the scene turned almost completely dark in front of me.

I didn't want to wake up. So, I said, "Change scene." It changed and I ended up at a place where a bunch of guys gathering up gears. They were going through a checkpoint, but I didn't have an ID badge. The guy at the checkpoint told me that there was a car waiting for me outside.

When I went out, I saw lots of large equipments, machines and robotics. I wanted to fly but I could only hover at lower altitude. As I was fading out again, I tried saying again, "Change scene." I also tried to do my spin.

Thereafter, I was going back and forth, between scenes too short to be remembered. At the transition state, the last image froze up. I tried to keep still to shift into another scene. Eventually, I just woke up. The session lasted for 30 minutes.

119-111712
SPIRAL TOTEM

The all-encompassing essence of my soul...

After 2 hours of meditation, I was at ease, stress free and felt as if I had a massage. I went back to bed. My wife was still in bed, and I learned not to let that hamper my out of body routine. I still maintained my focus on waiting for it. The signal came but weak, until I wanted to jump in to proceed with it. During the out of body phase, I was well aware of the presence of my wife and my physical body.

After the out of body phase, I was rolling, spinning, rotating and hovering all over the room. I was moving supinely feet first, hitting all parts of the room. When my feet reached the door, I gave it a little determination and I went right through the door. I was picking up speed going through numerous doors. I was calling out good words while going through.

Before long, I reached a wide-open expanse filled with stars, just like the universe. I wanted to do something. So, I used my finger to draw a spiral totem onto the universe, as if it was the canvas. I was aware that the totem meant emptiness, when I drew it. Some of the stars had irregular borders and they moved around.

My travel lost its direction and not going forward. Slowly, the scene changed, and I ended up with a bird's eye view looking down from very high up. In a very large open space, there were multiple groups of people congregated in patches of area. They all were fighting, screaming and seemingly hurting each other. People were hurt, bleeding and lying in sofas and chairs, sick and not moving. They looked very small while I was hovering over them. Suddenly, I just woke up. It's been only 10 minutes.

120-112112
MUD CREATURES

Unpleasant events do occur in the afterlife.

After meditation, I went back to bed. My wife was still in bed. At times, I felt her moving. Nevertheless, signal came and out of body movements occurred. I was out of the body floating supinely feet first all over the room, even right over my wife. I settled by the bed on the floor. I felt I wasn't doing anything.

While I was reciting the 9words Mantra, I put my hands above my head expecting going somewhere else. Immediately after, I was aware of being transported backwards through the glass door into another place. It was just a dark, ordinary room or corridor. I was feeling my way to the end, and I turned a doorknob. I opened the door and walked out to a wide-open space, like the landscape in a park or around a resort. I could see short shrubs with green leaves and shinny water droplets. I opened my eyes and the whole scene became so vivid and vibrant. I was both excited and happy.

While I was walking around with joy, I saw these big globs of mud creatures. They opened their bodies and moved slowly. I tried to jump around to avoid them. While I was enjoying the scene, they caught up with me and it was too late for me to change the scene. I felt they got ahold of my legs. I didn't intend to convert them, and I also didn't like how it felt. I struggled a little and just woke up.

121-112412
SELF PERSPECTIVES

━━━━━━━━━

The soul has no limitations on where to set its perspective.

After 2 hours of meditation, I went back to bed at 6:50 and my wife was still in bed. Shortly, jolts of signal were hitting me continuously. They came quick and went away just as fast. Then the intensity gradually increased along with shorter intervals between them.

With more concentration on the signal, finally one strong continuous signal during which I felt slight movement peeling away from the body. At first, I rolled to the right, then back to the left out of the physical body with my head leaving last.

As soon as I settled by the side of the bed, next to where the head of my sleeping physical body. I asked for clarity. Immediately after, I felt one of my eyes opened wide, seeing a circular, vivid, clear cropped out image of my bed from a distance. The funny part was that I also found my real eyes opened, looking at the things in the left corner of the room from the perspective of my physical sleeping position. I was quite perplexed that I was still able to see from my physical body after leaving the body. So, I closed my eye, and I ended up in that left corner of the room.

At the same time, I recited the 9words Mantra and brought both of my Dharma Seals together above my head, wanting to fly away. Apparently, I went through the roof hovering outside right above the house. But I couldn't recognize the exterior of the house. I thought about flying away in full speed and I did. In the middle of the universe, I was zipping through randomly all over the universe in lightning speed. The picture of the universe changed a few times.

When I stopped and paused, I got emotional and cried. I was touched and moved from marveling at all the worlds and people in all these infinite tiny sparkling dots. At that moment, I felt my consciousness being all over the universe and not just in me alone.

After that, I showed up in a furniture store where I was strolling through. Then I went through a false awakening showing 7:25 on the clock. At the end, I woke up at 7:11.

122-112512
A TOUCH OF REALITY

My soul every so often, could foretell what comes next.

After two hours of meditation, I went back to bed. Signals were weak and I slipped into unconsciousness. Then I awakened to find myself repeatedly touching the fabrics in a marketplace. It felt real with a touch of substance.

I also could see clearly my shirt sleeves in khaki color. From that point on, I became active. I was walking through the marketplace, touching everything.

Then I got restless, wanting to get out. I peeked through one of the stalls but there was no opening. Nevertheless, I already knew there was nothing outside of the marketplace.

Shortly, I ended up in the open trying to fly but I couldn't. There was something latched onto me tightly. Moment later, I flew away with two inanimate objects latching on my sides. When I looked out in the distance, it wasn't quite clear. I got the signal that I was done here. I woke up to a false awakening, where I stayed for a while before waking up.

123-112612
SLOW DETACHMENTS

_____

At times, my soul would show and tell in detail... _____

After meditation, I went back to bed lying on my left at 7:00. Signal came and gone. Finally, one lasted long enough and I began leaving the body. I rolled a little to the right and very slowly part by part detaching from my body.

Once I left the body, I stood upright by the bed near the door. As I was asking for clarity, I rushed out of the bedroom into the living room. From that point on, I took control. I started walking forward on my own towards the front door. I turned the doorknob, opened and walked out to the front yard. I looked up, it was dark and not clear. I asked for clarity but nothing changed.

Meanwhile, I tried to fly away but feeling heavy and anchored to the ground. During the process so far, I felt rushed and there was too much will on my part. I slowly faded out of there into the transition state where I was awakened lying in bed. And I was aware of this fade-out-fade-in shift which was seamlessly smooth with no lapses. The entire field of view in my mind slowly evolved into scattered black dots and patterns. I stayed put and apparently drifted into a dream state.

124-113012
SIMILAR BUT DIFFERENT

There's zero distance between my body and soul...due to the superposition of the two realms.

After meditation, I went back to bed in the bedroom. My wife was sleeping outside. Lately, I had discovered that lying on my left was putting some pressure on my heart and stomach. So, I tried lying on my back this time.

Signals and vibrations kept coming. When the strong one triggered the body separation process, I would roll slowly to the right til facing down. After I was completely separated from my body, I would gasp for breath due to breath holding over the separation phase. Often, I recoiled right back into my body, just like this time.

The second time around, I was focusing on some irregular patterns rearranging themselves in my mind. Finally, I was detached and stabilized as an immaterial entity.

Although I wanted to fly but I felt being trapped in my study room. I called for clarity but to no avail. I tried to walk through the wall and that didn't work. Instead, I ended up just simply opening the door and went outside. The hallway looked exactly like the physical one.

At that moment, I knew my wife was sleeping in the living room in real time. I found her sleeping in the larger sofa and she talked to me. I wanted to do something so that I could confirm it later after waking up. I put a small stuff animal on the armrest of the smaller sofa. The arrangement of the two sofas was the same as in the physical reality.

Moment later, I proceeded to go out to the front courtyard. I yelled out to my wife, "This does not look like my front yard." There was a very tall solid wall with vines growing all over the place. My wife said, "They are bay leaves not ivy." I walked out to the open and just wanted to fly away. I took a leap upward and flew around for a while. It wasn't very smooth, somewhat awkward.

During that time, I was making a loud noise from my throat. A woman asked me why I would make that noise. Then another man approached to talk to me. Suddenly, his image froze up and slowly faded away. I knew I was about to wake up. As the last image was fading away, I recited the 9words Mantra few times to show my appreciation for this wonderful experience. It was a session of 25 minutes.

Note: I later realized that I had mucus build up in my throat while lying flat on my back. I also found out later that my wife was actually sleeping in the smaller sofa instead, and there was no item on the armrest.

125-120112
ALIEN SPACESHIP

My body and soul can be separated in a flash.

After meditation, I went back to bed lying on my back at 7:01 am. My wife was also in bed. There was only a mild signal. My wife interrupted me few times and I gave up at 7:18 am.

I was just lying there about getting up to go to work. Suddenly, "Pow!", I was yanked out of my body horizontally, headfirst in the backward direction. I took off so fast that I was stunned but amazed, despite leaving the body so many times in the past 3 years. I was going at high speed. It felt like either something was pulling me, or an aircraft carrying me. For a moment, I told myself not to be frightened and just go with it, to see where it would take me. I also recited the 9words Mantra couple times.

As I was traveling through the open space, I was not look-ing at my surrounding, just focusing on the ride itself. When I opened my eyes to look, it seemed like I was cruising at low speed inside of a gigantic and expansive space station. I couldn't help but assumed it was an alien spaceship of some kind. The top flat ceiling was embossed with totems or sym-bols beyond my understanding. The whole place was dim with just one color of dark gray.

When I arrived at a room with a blanket over my face, feeling a bit out of breath. I did think that I might have accidentally put a blanket over my face in real time. Somehow, I knew it was my home but I couldn't recognize it.

I called out "Honey" instead of her name, because I knew she was not my real wife. When I entered the room, I saw her sitting with her back towards me. She stood up. I was surprised to see that she looked very similar to my real wife. But not exactly, she had short yellowish blond hair. I went over to talk to her and touched her face, feeling very close to her.

Then there were my two children, but I didn't take a good look at them. I asked them for the year we were in. They couldn't answer. I went all over the house looking at calendars but none with the year. For a moment, I thought this might be a parallel universe without the dating system. So, I couldn't really tell them that I was from another time.

When I looked out of the window, I saw heavy machinery, vehicles and log pile. I also noticed that the house was situated next to the beach, bay or port. I felt that I had seen this same scene in my previous out of body encounter. It really looked that familiar. I even went out to take a look. I asked the kids if they ever went out to the water.

When I went back in and asked about the year again, my aunt and my mom were there, and they had no idea what I was talking about. So, I went over to my wife and asked her, "Honey, what's your name?" She got upset and pulled out a small kitchen knife and attempted to cut herself to prove something. During the whole time, I was not as emotional as before. This time, I didn't shed any tears. When I tried to stop her, everything came to a sudden stop and faded away quickly. I woke up thereafter at 7:33 am. The session was only 15 minutes long but seemed very long.

126-120412
BUSY TRAVELING

It seems like I have never moved... just watching images come and go.

After two hours of meditation and extensive breathing practice, I went back to bed lying flat on my back. I was quite alert. There was no signal or vibration. Next moment, I just slowly slipped out of my body. I was hovering very closely over my body until I kept clearing my throat and woke up. Although I knew I didn't clear my throat before going to bed, but that turned out to be a false awakening.

Before long, I was flying again. This time, I wanted to fly through places and see things along the way, avoiding rushing to a place instantly. I called out, "Fly to China." As I was flying, I noticed something loud right on my tail and gaining on me. It passed me and crashed into a town. It looked like a train and robotic transformer with its machine parts scattered all over.

I was paying attention to it and those two stories' buildings around there. I said to myself, "All these looks real but they're actually the manifestation of my mind."

A while later, whole lot of people and kids came out for a car racing event. One of the kids kept ramming at me with his car. While I was holding him back, the parent was saying something to me. I just rose up like an elevator. I almost got tangled up with the power line.

Once cleared, I took off flying. I was thinking of Hawaii at the time. I saw a beautiful island with visible living areas, just like Tahiti from up high. But I kept flying with a sensation of pressure under my heels, as if I was standing or pushing against something solid. It was the same feeling I had when I rose up earlier.

In the next scene, I landed involuntarily at a residential area like Orange County in California, deserted but with funny looking trees. As I was walking through the area, it revealed a scene that I recognized from another out of body encounter. But at present, it was brighter and I was able to recognize few areas in the scene. All the while, there was this eerie sound playing, I wondered and pondered over what had I ever done here before. Shortly after, I woke up. It was a session of 30 minutes.

127-120512
DISJOINTED EVENTS

Every image in the afterlife seems to exist independently...
without the need for sequential support.

After meditation, I went back to bed lying on my back at 7:40 am. Upon a mild signal, I felt like being carried out of my body again. This time was to the left, headfirst horizontally but in a downward direction. I wondered if I was going to a more unpleasant place. Immediately, I started to recite the 9words Mantra.

Soon after, I was going through a large tubing facility where there were many white coat workers working. I was talking to a girl who had cancer and her family came to talk to her. I was with a scientist looking man whom I didn't recognize. He was talking about some surgical procedures.

Meanwhile, I felt a lot of pain in my gum near upper central incisors and upper lip area. Directly after, he took me to a facility to show me a model plane. He said it's made of aluminum. I noticed the front of the plane was square and not pointed. I also walked towards a warship of some kind. The front deck of the ship was open with a piece of something in the center and the rest was hollow and open. I said to myself that this must be the future design to cut through waves.

128-120612
PEOPLE EVERYWHERE

There're countless people and beings in the afterlife.

After meditation, I went back to bed lying on my back. My wife was also in bed sleeping and snoring. Nevertheless, I went ahead anyway to do my thing. I kept still and waited for signals which would come in between her snores.

To my surprise, instantly I was flying over densely populated small box like cities with a bird's eye view. I landed amid great many people on the city streets. I was able to hover and float through the streets couple feet off the ground. I could also cross my legs and levitate.

Shortly after, I would walk through the streets talking and interacting with people around. After a while, I wanted to check up on my real home. I asked a person to borrow his phone. I told him that I got mugged and I didn't have my wallet. He was dialing on a small table. I told him Pasadena. He hit 626 and I called out my real home phone number. It didn't go through. At that moment, I asked the same question once again, "What year is it?"

I saw couple calendars on the wall with no year. They didn't seem to know what it was. Later, I decided to ask some guys about their ages to find out how they calculated their ages. That didn't come through. I came back to the transition state couple times before heading back to the same scenes.

I was sitting at the head of a long table where others gathered around. We talked. There were a set of adult male twins, and a man joked about my race. I saw a cow constituted out of leaves and wood branches and I showed my surprise.

Then I asked a woman to my left, "How many suns do you have?" She said three. It was bright and sunny. I saw only one and looking for the other two. It was cloudy at other places, and I didn't see them. While I was flying over the city, I wanted to fly faster and away but not knowing where to go. It was a session of 25 minutes.

129-120712
HAPPY FLYING

My soul could also be in such a jolly, good mood.

After two hours of meditation, I went back to bed lying on my left. I showed up in a scene where I saw funny looking and undefined monster-like creatures in two directions. They walked away and came back towards me with their friends. I could sense that they were up to no good. I just stood up and took off straight up into the sky.

Meanwhile, I was hovering, flying and floating over the streets of a city. I was in such a jolly mood. After a while, I stared into the fog in front, but I couldn't see anything. And I still wanted to fly too somewhere else.

I picked Hawaii. I was diving through the clouds towards land of an island. When I landed on the rocks, I felt pain on my knees.

Then the scene changed. I was in a dark bedroom with a couple in the room sleeping. I walked out to a junk yard industrial place. When I came back to the house, I heard the couple talking. I got a feeling that the guy might be me in another world and I wanted to look at him. But he looked more like my brother. Later, he looked more like my older son at a much older age. I asked, "How old are you?". He was laughing and joking. I didn't look at the woman. I woke up with no false awakening. The session was 20 minutes long.

130-121212
WHO AM I

_____

My soul does not have a definitive look.   _____

After meditation, I went back to bed lying on my back. I was just toggling between unconsciousness and the transition state, where I focused on any image in my mind. From then, I would pick up some signals.

As I continued, the signal became strong enough to initiate the out of body movements. During the process, I couldn't relax due to my shortness of breath. At that moment, I realized that I was inhaling continuously to get across. Feeling out of breath, I drifted right back to the transition state. I didn't give up and I tried focusing again.

This last time was quick. Both signal and vibration were strong but no actual out of body movements, and bedroom scene was quick to follow. I just seamlessly crossed over to another scene where I remained in bed with raised blankets surrounding me. There was sound associated with it. The blankets were up high, and it was dim, so that I couldn't see anything. I asked to stop couple times. It stopped after a while but not right away. I couldn't make sense out of what I was shouting afterwards.

Suddenly, the scene in the apartment got lucid and vivid. I approached the window and opened it. I was at about 10-15 stories high. As I looked out, I saw a great number of white dwellings. I said, "It's like Greece." I wondered if I was in Greece. I looked around more and saw plenty of rubbles and collapsed buildings. There were people walking in between. In the meantime, I kept clearing my throat. I wanted to spit it out but worried about waking up.

As I walked towards the bathroom in the back of the apartment, I saw this light fixture following me like a little robot. I also saw a video camera on the desk. When I got to the bathroom, I turned around and looked at myself in the mirror of the medicine cabinet. I couldn't see the head, it was missing.

At that moment, I started to wonder if I had the same look as my real physical face. If not, how would I look like?

Shortly, there were some mirage-like images appearing in the mirror. I continued focusing on it until a young man's face appeared. It was very clear and vivid. He didn't look Chinese or Asian and it was difficult to determine his race. I just kept staring at him, trying to burn his image in my mind so that I won't forget. Slowly, it faded away and I woke up. It was a 30-minute session.

131-121912
STICKY FILAMENTS

Desire was also a part of my soul.   ———

After two hours of meditation, I went back to bed lying on my left. I found myself following a small toy like car which was moving forward. I touched it and pushed it. Meanwhile, I could just hover and move as I pleased, not feeling much of a body.

All sudden, I felt this surge of speed. I was flying upward and backward, feeling air rushing by me. I just let loose and flew all over the dark space. I saw countless of filament clusters floating around. I grabbed one which felt sticky on my hand. I tried to pull it off.

While up in the air, I said, "I want to go somewhere, how about Hawaii?" And I expected it to manifest right below me. I ended up in a house. At that instant, I felt this sudden sexual desire. I remembered that I could have it if I wanted it.

As I walked around the hallway towards the bedroom, I saw a couple laughing in bed. The guy just vanished. Everything just froze up and slowly faded away. I also woke up to a false awakening. Session was 30 minutes long.

132-122812
SIT UP AND LEAVE

___

Before my soul breaks away completely...the
perception of body remains.

___

I woke up late this morning and felt tired. After 60' of medita-tion, I went back to bed lying on my left. My wife was also in bed. I felt several signals but no follow through. Finally, I started to roll to the right, then immediately back to the left. I thought that was another failed attempt.

Surprisingly, I was separated from my body by practically just sitting up to get out of bed. I felt a strong force push-ing from behind. Instead of floating, I touched the floor and walked out of my room into the living room. It was dim and I asked for clarity but to no effect.

Right before I was about to get outside from the front door, I saw my wife sitting at the dining table. I went over to touch her and grabbed her hand. The contact with her hand felt real. Her features became quite vivid and clear. I saw tat-toos on her neck and front chest area. She was young and unlike my wife. As I tried to focus to remember, I woke up instead.

133-122912
FLY LIKE AN EAGLE

Visualization can override the apparent obstacles.

After 80' of meditation, I went back to bed lying on my left at 6:25 am. It was a very cold morning. My wife was also in bed with a cough. Signal was strong but the body separation phase lasted for a long time. I was aware of myself needing to stay focused, relaxed and gasping for breath after the crossover.

Directly after, I quickly walked out to the living room where the glass door was. I just visualized myself going through the glass slowly. Once out, I flew low and I turned around seeing the rooftop of my house. I continuously flew over the snow-covered treetops everywhere. I could even reach out and touched the snow on the treetops.

After I landed somewhere, I was looking at a person over a distance from me. That was the last image, froze up and faded away slowly. I woke up thereafter. It was a short session of 15 minutes.

134-010513
MY BODY'S MISSING

My body in the afterlife is nothing more than just an image.

After 60' of meditation, I went back to bed lying on my left. I was still recovering from a cold and stuffy nose. There were some signals but no vibration. A moment later, I just floated out of my body facing down. I was able to see my arms vividly, dangling in front of me.

The surrounding was very clear. First, I floated out of the room in a prone position and then back to my bed. I couldn't see my body in bed, but I saw my wife waving at me from her side of the bed.

Then I moved out into another scene where I wanted to fly but I couldn't. I felt something latching onto me around my hip and waist. I struggled with it and finally pried it off before I flew away. Session was 20 minutes long.

135-012513
CAN HAPPEN ANYTIME

My soul is the portal to the afterlife... a universal hub to all.

After a 30' meditation at night, I went to bed at 11:00 PM and feeling tired. This was one of those unusual experiences that happened at night. The neighbor was noisy. I lay down on my back. I was keeping my body calm and stlll, trusting something would emerge.

Upon the signal, I drifted out of my body and ended up resting on the floor. Then I proceeded to walk outside. Just when I was about to open the window to a vivid scenery. In a flash, I recoiled back into my physical body and woke up. I was guessing my wife might have either called me or yanked on the blanket. While I was waking up, I still had the last image intact in my mind. Afterwards, I drifted into regular sleep for the night.

HENRY C WONG

136-021213
CENTER OF THE EARTH

Hollow earth can undeniably exist in the afterlife.

After 60' of my early morning meditation, I went back to bed lying on my left side. Signals came but they were very subtle and faint. Nevertheless, I started out rolling a little to the right about 90 degrees but without the follow-through. So, I rolled back to the left. After few times of right-left back and forth rolling, I paused for a while. Shortly after, I was able to roll to the right to leave my body successfully.

Once I was out floating in a supine position, I was thinking, "Take me to the center of the earth." Immediately after, I picked up speed and moved with my head in front. I didn't think I was moving fast enough. I thought of light speed, or speed to that effect.

Just like that, I was apparently flying and floating inside of a gigantic enclosure. I didn't see any people or land that I recognized. But I saw plenty of undefined abstract objects and places. I did recognize a huge round opening with stars and image of the universe on the outside. I was flying towards the opening, but I didn't get out.

Shifting to the next scene, I ended up on land seeing bunch of inanimate objects all around. Finally, I saw a young woman and I asked her some questions. She told me this guy whom I seemed to know his name, was a lawyer and I was the clerk. I was somewhat disappointed that I was only a clerk. I saw a current day calendar displayed on the wall. I thought, "Not again, every time is the same thing. I ask and she doesn't know. It doesn't have the year." I didn't see the year and I couldn't read the rest of it.

Afterwards, I walked out to the open where a great number of people gathered around. I asked them where's the sun inside. They said it's getting dim. I also saw huge columns of man-made structures jutting out, falling and collapsing. I went back inside, feeling that I had spent too much time at this place already. I went back outside and flew straight up into the space. I couldn't see anything, just dark empty space. I woke up thereafter. It was a session of 20 minutes.

Note: I did not think of the center of the earth at all before the session.

137-021313
KINDNESS TO ALL

Real life self cultivation affects my soul just as much...

After 60' of meditation, I went back to bed lying on my left side. There was some noise distraction outside of the room. When I drifted into the transition state, my body was still and I was calm. I was being watchful over my mind. Not long after that, the body separation started. I couldn't see anything but just remembered the alarm going off in the hallway. I was getting confused whether I was awake or not. That was why I couldn't remember the details up to that point.

Suddenly, I saw a bunch of electrical wires and fixtures hanging down from the ceiling in the hallway. I told myself that my actual house didn't look like this. Once I realized I was in another realm, I became more at ease and less worried.

So, I asked to be taken to my next life. I went out to the open attempting to fly away, but someone was grabbing on my legs. Finally, I shook him off and flew away. I saw his very small body on the ground. I recited the 9words Mantra and directed my Dharma Seal upon him.

I flew out to the seaside where there were people gathering. I was chatting with a woman and some kids. Shortly after, the woman and I walked out to another place. As we were moving, I woke up. It all lasted 30 minutes.

138-021513
FATHERLY LOVE

---

*My soul's sentiment is eternally true only to the
associated moment.*

After 60' of meditation, I went back to bed lying on my left. My wife wasn't around in the room. I started first with seeing a young Asian woman, hinted Korean, sitting at the end of my bed. While we were talking, I left my physical body but the process was not as real as before. I floated up and landed on her. I did have a flash thought of making advances to her but I didn't.

She slowly changed into a young girl. Thereby, my feeling towards her had changed into a fatherly love. I was touching her face which was very clear and vivid, while she was still talking. I said to her that I wanted to go somewhere else. So, I held her hand and we both were walking through the door to the hallway.

At that moment, I heard the doorknob turning and instantly I woke up. After I became awakened in real time, and only then my wife turned the doorknob and opened the door into the room, apparently from a shower. It was a 15-minute session.

139-021913
FAMILY REUNION

My soul has great capacity to transcend parallel realities.

After 60' of meditation, I went back to bed lying on my left side. It was quiet and I was alone. I was drifting in and out of unconsciousness. At certain point in time, I was conscious that I paid attention to my third eye area to initiate something. I was aware that with my attention, images would form and continue their own. While images were forming, I swiftly left my physical body.

Out of nowhere, something was going under my armpits from behind. I ignored it and requested to go to a parallel universe. I did think about that request couple days ago during the day. There was no sensation of traveling.

The person behind, who hugged around my chest was my current wife. We both were looking out of the window at plenty of flowers. I asked her if they were our flowers. Promptly, our only two sons walked into our room. They both were big and grown-up. I said to myself that they must be my current family of tour, in another world of parallel universe. The rest afterwards was blurry, and I couldn't remember. The session was about 30'.

140-022013
ROAST DUCK

My soul hasn't experienced eating thus far.

After 50' of meditation, I went back to bed lying on my back. I was feeling at ease, so I turned to the left side. By merely concentrating on the third eye area during a fully awakened state, nothing would happen. As I slowly drifted into the transition state, half asleep state, I focused on the third eye area. Immediately, I just rolled to the right and separated from my body.

Then I walked out of the room feeling a strong push behind me. I opened the front door to the front yard which looked like my real yard. It was dark and I asked for clarity, and it got a little brighter.

Meanwhile, I had to free my right arm from an entangled blanket before I could fly. Once freed, I elevated up slowly into the air. I asked to be taken to the moon. Shortly, I ended up in a place inside of a spacecraft of some kind. I heard my old classmate's voice but I ignored it and walked away.

Abruptly, I was strolling along the streets where people going about their business. I saw Chinese characters on signs in front of the stores. I also saw ducks hanging in the stores. I was thinking of eating a piece to see how it would taste.

I walked by a woman and I squeezed her arm. I also thought of finding myself a good-looking woman to talk to, but no luck.

I ran into some westerners sitting at a table. I approached one of the kids and asked him where he was from. He said something that I couldn't understand. He said a place that I didn't know. When I asked him, "What's this place?" He gave me some name like Hawaii. Then I tried to climb up the building using skills that I thought I had. But I was struggling until I woke up. It was a session of 25 minutes.

141-022113
A MUNDANE SESSION

My soul does have choices on occasions in the afterlife

After 60' of meditation, I went back to bed lying on my left side. My wife was also in bed. From dreams I drifted into the transition state. When I focused at the images in the third eye area, signals came, and I started rolling slowly to the right. The process was not swift. When I detected a little disturbance from my wife, it came to a halt. I didn't give up and tried again.

This time, I didn't go to the right but instead, rolling to the left side right off the bed to the floor. I immediately popped back up kneeling on the floor. I heard noise coming from my wife's direction, apparently, she was still in bed. I quickly opened the bedroom door, but I felt a great deal of resistance.

When I walked out into the living room, I asked to see an old friend of mine. Nevertheless, I woke up at that point from this 25-minute session. After yesterday's mundane session, I decided to do more experiments.

142-030913

DA ZI ZAI WAN FO

Every journey is basically unknown to my soul.

After 45' of meditation, I went back to bed lying on my left side. My wife was also in bed. As I relaxed, I was aware of the slightest rolling movement to the right, but not coming from my physical body. It was like telling yourself to do something but it's not your body that was doing it.

When I encouraged the rolling movement the second time, I felt the vibrations, not very strong but distinct. As the rolling moved more to the right, I felt my self-awareness gradually shifted from my physical body into the rolling movement itself. Subsequently, I rolled back to the left facing down and off the bed, completely separated from my body.

However, I couldn't stop spinning around my own vertical axis. I called on myself to stop spinning. It worked and I immediately asked for clarity. It also cleared up and I quickly walked out of the room through the hallway to the living room. Unexpectedly, I was feeling grateful and thanked Buddha "Da Zi Zai Wan Fo" at that moment.

I kept walking out of the house to the front gate which should be locked in my physical world. However, I opened it, and it was not locked. When I was outside of the gate, there was a lot of commotion, but I didn't see anybody. When I heard a distinct sound right next to me, I knew I was going back. I did try not to think of my body but to focus on the scene to stay longer. Apparently, it didn't work, and I woke up thereafter. Session was 20 minutes long.

143-032313
BRIGHTER FREQUENCY

Apparently, my soul knows about frequency.

After dreaming during the meditation, I got a sore neck and upper shoulders. I also had a sore throat at the time. I went back to bed lying on my back. I didn't expect anything, just wanted some more sleep and rest. My wife was also in bed. I was not aware of when exactly, I drifted into the transition state.

From there, I just popped out of my body and floated supinely. I showed up in a different place other than my bedroom. It was an apartment in a high-rise building. Immediately, I was anxious and wanted to do something quickly. I called out, "Stand up." Nothing happened right away. So, I called out for clarity. While I was standing up right, the scene also got clearer.

Right after, I walked around a little and asked to be taken to a higher frequency. Instantly, the scene became even brighter, vivid and colorful. I didn't really know what to expect. However, when I got outside in the open, it was dark and undefined. As I was flying into the open, I woke up to a false awakening. My office assistant was telling me that there were these large creatures and fish people. I told her that I had seen them before and recorded in my journal. Gradually, I woke up once again.

144-032513
DANCING TO THE MUSIC

<hr>

My soul has shown me who I truly am.

After 30' of meditation, I went back to bed lying on my back. Due to my stuffy nose from a cold, I switched back to the left side. It didn't take long before I could feel the rolling to my right. Then quickly, I rolled back to my left where I felt the separation from my body. I found myself standing in the corner of the room, not wanting to rush into anything. However, I was aware of being very close to my body which could pull me back prematurely.

When I asked to be taken outside, I felt this sudden "shooting through a tube" feeling right away. I ended up in an unfamiliar room which was lively and vivid. I was looking at my two real looking hands. I even made Dharma Seal and few other gestures.

At the same time, I heard noises from the outside that resembled my real-life environment. I was thinking that I could be in both realms at the same time. I looked out of the window and I saw numerous old-fashioned bicycles on the street as in China several decades back. I was saying to myself that this is not how my outside supposed to look like.

I walked out to an unfamiliar living room. I asked for clarity couple times and it got vividly clear. I was happy and dancing a bit with some music in the background. Suddenly, I just woke up from it at 7:15. I did plan on getting out of bed at 7:15 after meditation.

145-033113
PUSH-UP WITHIN

―――――

My soul operates from a cumulative perspective, rather than just revolving my current life.   ―――――

There was no meditation this morning. After the recitation of the 9words Mantra, I went back to bed lying on my left side. I had an ear plug in my right ear due to my wife's heavy breathing. Signal came and I somehow ended up facing down, but remained in my body. I proceeded to push up against my body with both hands as in a push-up exercise. Right away, I was separated from my body.

Straightaway, I felt very confident and assertive. Right after I told myself to stand up, I just shot up standing but hovering about 3 feet off the floor. After asking for clarity couple times, the scene in the bedroom was as clear as the real one.

My wife was still in bed at that time and I didn't approach her. Unexpectedly, I went ahead to use my right hand doing a swipe gesture to make her disappear. Shortly after, she just vanished.

Later, I asked to be taken to the center of the earth again. There was no rushing sensation, and I felt I wasn't going anywhere. But I found myself in an unfamiliar building. Afterwards, I just woke up from this 25-minute session.

146-040113
FAMILIES EVERYWHERE

My soul attested to countless sentimental memories in my past.

After meditation, I went back to bed. Signal came and I came out of the body quickly. I was floating around a bit in the room. Suddenly, my legs straightly pointed up towards the ceiling, where there was an opening to the blue sky. My feet got outside of the opening but my body wasn't following through. I got impatient not willing to wait for what could happen next. I tried to will my body through but it didn't happen.

Soon after, I stayed back in the room wanting to pay more attention to the details of the scene. As I looked out of the window, I saw a neighborhood of houses, but I noticed they were slanted, run-down and not upright. That raised a red flag.

Then I walked around the house and asked my wife, "How many kids do I have?" She said, "Two grownups and two young kids."

I noticed beds in several rooms. I also asked what kind of car she drove. I ran into her in the hallway. She was young and pretty, dressed up and ready to go to work. Slowly, I faded out of the scene.

From nowhere, I woke up to a false awakening in bed. But this one involved a lot of sheets and blankets floating up and around. I started to think there might be some evil interference. I immediately began reciting the 9words Mantra.

Before long, I found myself in another house greeted by two unfamiliar women. As I was looking at the older one, she looked Korean and supposedly the mother. The younger daughter was telling me that we had been married for 6 years after my divorce. I asked her, "Where are we?" She showed me a little hill and snow outside of the window. She held my hand and showed me around the house.

Afterwards, I went outside, and I saw a military parade. I was able to barely hover off the ground but couldn't fly away. So, I walked around somehow back to the house earlier. I felt I was being chased, thereby I woke up to another false awakening.

In this scene, I thought I had been traveling out of my body for a long time. There was a note from a doctor along with some Chinese medicines. A kid who was supposed to be my son, seemed reluctant to approach me to tell me that I had been gone for a long time. He looked worried. When he showed me the backyard of the house, I asked if it was ours. He said yes.

Suddenly, I realized that I was still traveling, and I burst into tears. I was deeply moved by the interconnection between all beings. And finally, I woke up to my actual physical reality. It was a long 40-minute session.

147-053113
TIBETAN CONNECTION

Magical manifestation in the afterlife...

After meditation, I went back to bed lying on my left side. When I initially visualized rolling to the right, I felt my physical body doing it. Gradually, I felt myself getting lighter and continuously rolling to the right over my wife.

Thus, the physical body was left behind. I raised my feet to a supine position with my head in the lead. As I was circling around the room to the bedroom door, I looked at my bed to see if my body was still there. Although everything was quite clear, I didn't see my body.

In an instant, I showed up at a place where there was blue sky, streets, people and buildings. Apparently, I was in a car like enclosure looking out. It was vivid and I wanted to focus on the blue sky to confirm that it was as real as the physical world. Meanwhile, I saw a woman in Tibetan clothing. She seemed surprised seeing me and avoided me. I saw another woman with a man, they acted the same way.

Without stopping, I got out into the open and just wanted to try out something. I saw a long path in front of me at a distance and there were people along that path. I pointed and directed my finger along the length of the path, visualizing a fire. I didn't see the fire, but I did see a wide band of bright orange color appearing over the path. Right away, I was concerned about disrupting people on that path.

Promptly, I pointed my two index fingers up into the open blue sky in two opposite directions. In no time, I saw a beam of white light forming an arc connecting my two index fingers' tips. When I brought my right finger to meet with my left finger, the white beam formed a circle on my left fingertip. Shortly after, I just woke up.

148-060813
MY SOUL MATE

My soul mate is someone I see a lot in the afterlife.

After meditation, I went back to bed lying on my left side. Slowly I felt myself rolling to the left off the bed so that I won't wake up my wife. As I was walking out of the bedroom, I found my wife right behind me.

As soon as I got to the living room, the scene suddenly cleared up and became more vivid. I didn't want to get caught up by my wife, so I walked quickly to the front door and out of the house. When I got through the front gate out to the driveway, there was a cut down tree lying there. I jumped onto it and felt the softness of the leaves. At that time, I saw my wife also out of the house. I woke up thereafter. It was a 15-minute session.

149-060913
SENSATION OF ZERO GRAVITY

My soul could bring about a sensation that I, the physical body, had never experienced before.

After meditation, I went back to bed lying on my left side. It didn't take long before I rolled to the right. At first, I thought I was physically rolling and touching my wife because I saw my body. After I rolled back to the left, slowly I realized I was leaving my body and going around the room. I could see my body and my arms crossed against my chest the whole time.

As I approached the bedroom door, I thought of being taken to see my childhood friend. Immediately after, I felt the take off and rushing through the air. A while later, I found myself in a place where there's a whole lot of people and commotion amid some kind of ceremony. I was going through the place just looking for my friend. I kept moving out of that place into the streets. I was scouting for her.

From afar, I saw a woman looking like her approaching me. As she got closer, there was this large white encasing with two large openings blocking me and strangely with me inside of it. I just couldn't get to see her up close. I was asking for more clarity continuously as I walked through the assembly.

Even though it had become very clear and vivid, I got bored. I did my spin on a wide street for another scene. I was thinking of going to the moon again.

Before long, I ended up in a room without gravity. First, I was fixing my left slip-on shoe that was coming off. I felt the sensation of no gravity. I even ran a little and did a front somersault and landed on my feet.

Without a pause, I proceeded to check out other rooms. I looked out of the window and saw fake looking houses. I also saw spacecrafts parked out there. I thought I had seen all these before. Suddenly, I just woke up. It was a 20-minute session.

150-062213
A NIGHT OUT

Experience from the physical world serves as my soul's cumulative reference.

After 30' of meditation, I went back to bed lying on my left side. There was no signal. However, I began rolling to the right, then rolled back to the left off the bed resulting in a sitting position. I again switched to the supine position with my two legs straight out to the front, floating out to the hall-way and front door. The whole-body separation process was so quick that I could have been confused, feeling still in the physical reality.

At the front door, I opened it and went out. I remembered seeing the white gravel rocks in the front court area. From there, I just rose straight up, hovering and overlooking the mountain landscape. There were plenty of lighted houses on the hillsides all around my home. And finally, I was able to see the rooftop of my house but it wasn't all that clear. I felt my eyes were stuck shut and I tried to open them with my hands.

The sky was full of dots as in the picture of the universe. Suddenly, I just flew swiftly into the sky but without any des-tination. It was a 15-minute session.

151-071313
FRACTAL TOTEMS

Great wisdom is required to decipher the existential revelations.

After 60' of meditation, I went back to bed lying on my left side. My wife was still in bed. I started rolling to the right and I might have pushed it a little too much. Again, I rolled back to the left until I left the body. As I was floating out, I thought of my past life. Immediately, I felt some changes around me and I knew I was going towards "It".

On the wall at the lower right corner of the room, I saw totems of characters and scripts. I couldn't recognize any of them. I even stood right in front of them and tried to make some sense out of them but no luck. The image was very clear at the time. All the totems were arranged within the shape of a teardrop which came into a gradient of sizes. Smaller teardrops constituted bigger teardrops, so on and so forth. At the time, I interpreted them as the shape of an explosion.

When I looked out of the window to the right, I saw a vast landscape of unidentifiable dome shape explosions everywhere. There were jade looking short square bars randomly everywhere under those explosions. As the explosions progressed, those bars got wiped out.

I questioned, "Is this the end of the world?" I was right next to one of these transparent explosions, thinking that I could be wiped out just as well. I felt I should move away from the area. I saw more of those marble looking bars everywhere outside. Slowly, the scene froze, and I woke up. It was a 15-minute session.

152-072513
REMEMBRANCE OF THE PAST

*It appears that my soul is predetermined to
do certain things.*

After 2 hours of meditation, I went back to bed lying on my left side. I was a lot more relaxed than usual. I pictured a soothing and uplifting feeling. I slowly and gently initiated a little rolling to the right. I was able to see my body rolled to its back, but simultaneously I also saw myself wearing dark blue pants.

Without a pause, I continued to float up supinely. While I was floating, I already prepared myself what to say, either "Clarity" or "Past life." As I floated around the room, I asked to see my past life and waited for it to happen. I saw some cartoonish scene and said to myself, "This can't be it."

Suddenly, I thought of my Teacher. When I was reciting the 9words Mantra, I wasn't as precise as I ought to be with every word. But I was happy, feeling a sense of accomplishment. I was able to remember my Teacher and the 9words Mantra even in this nonphysical realm. Shortly, the doorbell woke me up. It was a 20-minute session.

153-072813
THE MILKY WAY

━━━━━━━━

The existence is full of surprises.

During the 2 hours of meditation, I stumbled into a perception that I was completely empty without any image of myself meditating. I could see only the cushion and I was no where to be found. I had no body awareness, no pain or discomfort, not here or there. I was aware of my posture being erect and straight. When I had an itch on my face, I would dwell on my emptiness more and it would slowly go away. Although I opened my eyes to look at the clock with 25' more to go, I could quickly go back to the state of emptiness.

Afterwards, I went back to bed lying on my left. My wife was just leaving for work. When I was aware of being in the transition state, I started nudging to my right. After a few times, I left my body and floated around the room.

I was also reciting the 9words Mantra at the same time. It was dark and I asked for clarity. It cleared up a bit. Since I didn't want to just float around in the room, so I asked to be taken to the Milky Way. Instantly, I rose up faster and faster. Gradually, the stars of the universe started to appear all around me.

As I was moving forward, I entered the "Milky Way" supposedly. The initial scene of bright lights, myriads of patterns and majestic images shocked me, overwhelmingly stunned me. I was in disbelief and yet being grateful for the chance of seeing it. It continued for a while. I also saw countless crystal-like formations and patterns all around me. I was just taking it all in with great admiration.

Before long, I landed in a Chinese neighborhood. I was just walking around seeing people working, cleaning a man-made pond with water plants under a building. I said that the water was clean. I also attempted to fly off to see my childhood friend but that didn't work.

Suddenly, the scene changed. I was staring at the rear of a black car parked in front of a stand-alone European mansion, which was situated in the snow of a mountain. As the car sped off in the snow, I followed it closely. After a while, I felt like I was racing with it down the hill. The chase lasted for a while. Out of nowhere, I saw two small convertible sports cars flipped and rolled off to the side of the road. I just thought this might be something that would happen in the future, a telltale sign. A Chinese person told me this's Hamburg and I knew it's in Germany. I was just waiting for the police.

Someone told me about my friend Donnie in a martial art school. I went over to see him. I recognized him as the famous action star but only much older. We shook hands and I got emotional. He wanted to take a picture of us. Then he went to look for someone. I was waiting and slowly woke up thereafter. It was a 20-minute session.

154-080213
REALITY CHECK

Without comparison, experience is reality.

During the 2 hours of meditation, my upper left back was tired and restless. I was struggling to finish my second hour. Afterwards I went back to nap on the floor mats in my study room due to my wife's cough. I was lying on my left. The room was bright and not sure if I could calm down.

When I did feel the signal, my wife knocked on the door and came in trying to wake me up. She was kneeling and facing me while I was lying on my left side. I tried to ignore her and she later left. I got up being really upset because I didn't want to be bothered in the future.

I went to wash up and prepared to go to work. There were some very vivid small blue flowers behind the sink. Instantly, I started questioning the scene and wondered if I was in a dream.

As I walked out to the marketplace, everyone was as real as they could be. I even said to myself that in the physical world, only the person you focused on was clear and the peripheral would be blurry. It's also like that in the nonphysical realm. In that case, how could I tell the difference, whether I was in a dream or not? I woke up thereafter. Session was 20 minutes long.

Note: My wife never came into my study room on that day.

155-080413
TUNNEL VISION

My soul's version of the "Tunnel Experience" ...

After 70' of meditation, I went back to bed lying on my left. At first, I drifted into a dreamy state. From there, signal came, and I flowed with the out of body phase. I was carried straight up, into clouds of indescribable colors, with the backdrop of the universe and galaxies. Hidden in the empty space, I saw an expansive universe with stars and endless arrays of celestial bodies. I was whizzing through space at lightning speed, elated and grateful.

Thereafter, I was going through a colorful tunnel. It was not dark, showing texture patterned wall. It reminded me of my Teacher's lecture on the tunnel of the afterlife. While I was going through the tunnel, I saw a bright round white light at the lower right corner of my field of vision. I attempted to take a direct look at it but instead, I concentrated on going through the tunnel.

Suddenly, everything slowed down and the tunnel gradually became narrower and more constricted. At the same time, it looked like water flowing in. I started to get this out of air, out of breath and suffocating feeling. I didn't panic and I saw that as a test of my poise and equanimity. I managed to stay calm and collected.

Quickly, the whole scene opened into a river. Slowly, I floated towards the shore where there were people with their docked boats. They looked happy helping with the boater ahead of me. When it was my turn, I said, "I'm from San Marino." Suddenly, the scene froze, and I became awakened in other dreams before I woke up. It was a 20-minute session.

156-080813
BUDDHIST SYMBOL

A pleasant surprise...

After 2 hours of meditation, I went back to bed lying on my left. I didn't feel the leaving of my body. However, I was aware of myself floating in a room.

I had a large, donut-shaped thing around me. It occupied the room, preventing me from flying or going anywhere. I started reciting the 9words Mantra. I also pointed my right Dharma Seal at that thing. Slowly all the obstacles disappeared, and I saw clearly the clockwise Buddhist Symbol "Wan".

After breaking free, I drifted into other dreams with people that I didn't recognize. Session was about 20' long.

157-081213
INNER WHITE LIGHT

Experience repeats itself.

During the meditation, I was restless and struggling in the second hour. I went back to bed lying on my left even though I was running late. It was 7:16 and I had to be at work at 8:00. Mentally I was pressed for time, but I went ahead anyway, waiting for the signal. Although the signals were strong but no follow through, possibly due to the anxiety from the time constraints.

At one time, I kept still and held my breath, it went far but failed with me gasping for breath afterwards. After several failed attempts, I decided to just stay calm and roll with it without holding my breath. It worked and I floated out of my body to a dark room. I got bored after floating for quite a while. I wanted to go somewhere else but not knowing where.

Shortly after, I was going through a glass door into a very large dark room, the size of an auditorium. I was just floating around. Suddenly, I just started to recite the 9words Mantra and pointed both Dharma Seals outward to the open. I saw here and there clusters of filaments like chains of bacilli bacteria.

I also had noticed there was a very bright white light, the size of a flashlight right in front of me. I tried but couldn't block it with my hand. Apparently, the light was much closer to me. I was thinking it might've come from within me or simply just part of me.

Shifting to the next scene, I found myself flying along the arctic water with icy crystal mountains all around. I saw submarine like objects coming out of the water. My flying was losing altitude at times. I had this feeling that I had been out for too long and the urgency to go back. I found a quiet place to wake up to go back but someone there disturbed my attempt.

Meanwhile, I saw a big explosion and I flew over to take a look. When I landed there, I saw Asian looking soldiers in combat gears, but they also had monks clothing underneath. I also saw a great number of WWI type of tanks and military vehicles around. I made eye contacts with some of them. Suddenly, the scene froze, and I woke up. It was a 15-minute session.

158-081813
UPSIDE DOWN

The afterlife does not always respond to what my soul wants.

After meditation, I went back to bed lying on my left. During the transition state, I rolled to the right few times and eventually separated completely from my body. I floated my feet upward and turned vertically upside down.

At the same moment, I heard noise from my wife coming into the room. I ran into her while I was upside down. While I was floating around, I wanted to go to see an atom. This was on my mind right before coming to bed. Immediately after, I saw an abstract water-color painting of a large shrimp. I wouldn't think it was the inside of an atom.

Then I looked out of the glass door. There was a large backyard with plenty of willow trees and greens. I went outside and it turned into a seashore with many small blocks of dwellings, lining up along the shore. I asked for clarity, and it got more vivid. I looked back at my house; it was gray and small among all the others. My wife supposedly was also there.

I flew up and towards the more inland part of the house, wondering how it looked like. I couldn't get a clear picture of the front because of multiple blocks of housing extended as far as I could see. It was a 15-minute session.

HENRY C WONG

159-082213
FACES OF THE INFINITY

Secret of the existence occasionally reveals itself.

After meditation, I went back to bed lying on my left. During the transition state, I saw a multitude of images with patterned formations. Signals came a few times causing me to roll within my physical body, and ultimately separated from the body.

Without a break, I drifted into a scene where I saw a face morphing into other faces at high speed. It continued for a while. It went so fast that I couldn't remember or recognize any one of them.

160-090213
CONNECTED BUT INDEPENDENT

In the absence of time, images are disjointed and independent.

After meditation, I went back to bed lying on my left. My wife was also in bed. It was a holiday. I was wide awake and not getting anywhere at first. I felt the subtle signal and I knew it would come. I felt myself rolling slowly to the right. It stalled a bit before rolling back to the left. Then I just followed it until I rolled off the bed. I stood up and walked around asking for clarity.

Slowly, my feet lifted off the floor and I started floating around the room.

I saw my wife in bed but not clearly. Yet, I couldn't see my own body. I had this exhilaration and confidence after rolling off the bed. I floated to my sons' room. I rubbed their heads hoping they could remember when I woke up. I even knocked over their alarm clock on the dresser as a sign. At that time, everything was not vividly clear.

I went to the living room and flew straight up through the roof to the sky. The scene of the sky cleared up into a high-definition vivid picture with unfamiliar patterns and images. I was just soaking it all in. I woke up thereafter.

Note: My sons had already been living on their own for many years.

161-091313
BREATHING IN THE NONPHYSICAL

Breathing, a perspective not valid in the afterlife...

After meditation, I went back to bed lying on my back. Signal came but I felt like I was holding my breath. I was concerned if the body separation was fast enough.

However, I slowly just sat up and left the body quickly with a little push. As soon as I gasped for my breath, I recoiled back into the body. Afterwards, I drifted into unconscious dreams instead.

162-091413
WHERE'S MY ALTAR

Belief and faith are deep in my soul.

After meditation, I went back to bed lying on my left. My wife was also in bed. Despite all the disruptions from her, I managed to complete a body separation process after numerous attempts.

After floating for a while in the room, I walked out to the living room but not knowing where to go. All sudden, I thought of reciting the 9words Mantra. I went into my study room, and I didn't see my altar. Instead, I saw a wall of undefined, brownish, pitted and irregular wood carvings, not of anything that I knew. I woke up afterwards.

163-091913
A PRECIOUS EXPERIENCE

My soul has given me the validation of my faith.

After 60' of meditation with breathing practice, I went back to bed lying on my back. My left foot felt the cramp, so I rolled to my usual left side. Without much signal, I had already left my body floating around the room.

Slowly, I was going through the glass. In front of me, I saw a great expanse of mountain ranges and peaks. I was flying through them high and low, navigating around the peaks like a jet plane. In no time, I found myself in outer space, seeing all sorts of celestial bodies, constellations and various geometric images of light. I was just simply overjoyed and whizzing all over the space around me.

When I approached a very large Figure. He moved away from me. Eventually, there was a false awakening before I woke up. It was a 20-minute session.

164-092113
A RAINY NIGHT

A subtle awakening can shatter the perception of current reality.

After 45' of meditation, I went back to bed lying on my left. Signal came and I rolled out of my body off the bed. I was floating standing-up around the room. It was much brighter and clearer than usual, but I asked for clarity anyway. While I was floating about where my body should be, I didn't see any body.

Meanwhile, I attempted to will myself straight up and out of the room, but it didn't work. I did think of the moon, but I wasn't really committed to any place. So, I simply just opened the glass door and walked out to the backyard. Again, I tried to fly but I couldn't.

Apparently, it was nighttime, dark and rainy. I was levitating in a supine position over the grass. I could feel the rain coming down on me. When I saw my black shoes, I said to myself that I didn't have shoes like those. Only then, it dawned on me that I had been treating everything as the actual reality. It was that vivid and real. I couldn't differentiate it from my physical world.

After all that, I managed to fly straight up to the sky, but I couldn't make up my mind on where to go. So, I just idled in the middle of the sky. I woke up thereafter. It was a 15-minute session.

165-100113
DETACHMENT OF BODIES

*My new-found appreciation... my soul's
support for my physical body.*

After 60' of meditation, I went back to bed lying on my left. I drifted into lucid dreams where I wanted to leave my body. Then I found myself back into my bedroom scene. This time, I found myself facing my physical body and yet still within it. When I initially started to push off, I could feel my whole being including my physical body lifting off the bed. Gradually, I was feeling myself detaching from the underlying body. The sensation this time was quite real and pronounced.

Once completely out, I was floating supinely into other rooms with my feet in the front. I asked for more clarity, and it got more clear and brighter. Then I stood up but still gliding slightly off the floor. I saw bicycles in every room. My wife was walking around in the meantime. I called her and she looked back, with a similar look as my wife. That scene froze up and I woke up afterwards. It was a 15-minute session.

166-100813
MEETING MY TEACHER'S TEACHER

___

*The afterlife can provide situations not
feasible in the physical world.*

___

After 60' of meditation, I went back to bed lying on my left. I drifted into the transition state where I saw scattered images. I did make a conscious calling for an out of body experience in my mind. I tried to roll out from the right but stalled. Then I rolled back to my left until I was completely separated from my body. This time, the whole process was quite fast.

While I was levitating over the edge of my bed, I was startled that I was about to fall from a super high place. Thereafter, the images were hard to maintain. They didn't last as long, seemingly unstable, incomplete and unrecognizable.

At times, I was facing not much of anything, just blank and empty, at best some scattered little figments of images. I realized that I needed to create them, think about them otherwise there wouldn't be anything.

Shortly after, I was running through a corridor and even 90 degrees on the wall. Next moment, I was sitting in front of an altar like area with unfamiliar small statues. Then my

Teacher's Teacher adorned in yellow golden color, walked out and sat down on the altar. I immediately went to pay my respect to Him.

After that, it was harder and harder to remember all those unfamiliar images. Nevertheless, I was clear on what I was thinking. Without my thoughts, there wouldn't be much of anything.

Note: My Teacher's Teacher passed away about 20 years ago. I was also thinking during the detachment from my body that I should engage into more things in the physical world, such as art, science and places. So that I can have more to create in my mind and ultimately in my surroundings.

167-101413
A.D. AND B.C.

Repeated habits and tendencies had defined my soul.

After 40' of meditation, I ended early due to my bowel movement. I went back to bed lying on my left. I drifted into the transition state unconsciously. From there I woke up and began nudging slightly to the right. It just happened without the whole out of body process.

I simply found myself in a room with a woman. Everything looked very clear and vivid. She was not good looking. The color on her arms was white but dark color on her face. I called her over for a closer look. At that moment, I felt the sudden desire to approach her. But somehow, I just felt it was not right to do that. So, I left her.

A while later, I was cruising around the marketplaces and watching different people that I couldn't recognize. I found myself flying away from everything. I could either flying in the scene or thinking of a destination and being there instantaneously. I was looking up the sky, the universe, with all the stars and constellations. I was trying to decide on which one to fly to. In the end, I couldn't decide so I stayed put.

The scene around me changed into a loud place where people were eating and talking. There was a big screen showing something. I could only remember A.D. and B.C. but no numbers before or after them.

The setting resembled the ancient Roman times. I also saw celestial beings of all kinds moving about high up in the atrium which opened to the sky. I went outside and there was a pool party. I wanted to see how the water felt in this realm. It felt like the real thing.

Shortly, I went into a corner in a kitchen with pots and pans. There was a man who came in cooking his food trapping me in that corner. We were talking but I couldn't move away. Suddenly, I felt it was over and I woke up afterwards. It was a 20-minute session

168-101513
PARALLEL REALITIES

Experience confirms different versions of reality.

After 40' of meditation, I went back to bed lying on my left. During the transition state, I nudged to the right and immediately, I was lifted out of my body. I was floating supinely and spun around a bit. I actively opened my sight, and it was very clear and vivid.

Without a pause, I went out to the middle courtyard where the bamboo was. I stepped over the cut bamboo which I did over the past weekend. They felt like real bamboo.

Then I went up to the brick wall fence. I sat there and looked around. Everything was quite clear, vivid and colorful. I stood up and walked along the narrow top of the wall. When I was about to fall off, I wasn't worried, I just flew away.

I was flying at very low altitude and slow enough to check out the neighborhood. I stopped at a restaurant where I saw a couple. I asked about the place and the man didn't give me a straight answer.

As I flew around again, I saw the moon and I wanted to fly there. A short lapse thereafter, I found myself lying in a loud bar restaurant with a bunch of people. I woke up afterwards. It was a 15-minute session.

Note: The courtyard, bamboo and brick wall were the same as in my physical home.

169-102713
INSENSATE PINCHING

Sensations cannot be imagined or described.

After 60' of meditation, I went back to bed lying on my left. I wasn't sure if I had already drifted into the transition state. However, I nudged myself to the right and just kept rolling off the bed on that side.

That was my wife's side, and she was there hovering over me. I broke away and quickly glided out of the room, without stopping, out of the front door. I was just so anxious to get away.

When I was in the yard outside, it was very foggy and misty. Later, in that morning after I woke up, it was also very foggy and misty. I saw some bright landscape, like a town or city from far away. I was flying towards it. I met a young black girl, and she told me it's Los Angeles.

I was flying a lot this time. I told myself to spend more time to observe details and seek something interesting to do. I looked at flowers closely. I ran through a large glass door and a large flat screen TV. I was concerned of the electronics inside messing me up.

After a while, I did get a feeling of being out too long. When I woke up with a whole lot of people and family around me, I pinched my arm and leg but I couldn't feel anything. I knew I was still out and about. So, I went over to a quiet corner and attempted to sleep to wake up. A moment later, I woke up. It had been 40 minutes.

170-102913
OUR DAUGHTER SOMEWHERE

The immaterial aspects of the existence are just as real as the physical.

After 60' of meditation, I went back to bed lying on my left. I didn't know when I left the body. Suddenly, I was in my own dark bedroom. I walked to the hallway where I turned on the switch for the light. I knew I was in another realm. I was quite sure that the light connected to the switch won't come on as bright as in the physical world. It did come on very dim. just a spot of faint light from above.

Meanwhile, I walked out to the living room seeing my wife. She was sitting at her desk with her back towards me. I slowly approached her wondering if she would look like my wife. Yes, she did look like my wife and I recognized her.

We both walked into my study room. There was a bed and some unknown equipments. We were looking for our daughter. In my physical world, we never had any other children but our two sons. My wife was unwrapping bundles of clothes, but no baby found. I woke up thereafter.

171-110313
MY GUARDIANS

Faith comes from repeated validations.

After 40' of meditation and breathing practice, I went back to bed lying on my left. From consciousness to unconsciousness, then again, I woke up in the transition state where I was able to will myself out of the body. It happened very fast without any delay and obstruction.

I stood up and levitated few feet off the floor and going all over the house. This time, the process was a little different. As I was leaving the body, I had less touch sensation but the visual was clear, as if I was seeing through my eyelids.

The floating around stopped suddenly in my study room. I was looking at a sit-down statue of a Guardian of Dharma, who had a sword worn across his waist. He reminded me of one of the eighteen Sangharama Bodhisattvas but without a beard. Slowly, he changed into all different figures.

Afterwards, there was a boy taking me around. I looked out of the window. There were some constructions next door, and I tried to focus on the details. At times, I called out for more clarity to see better. I saw my wife and gave her a hug. Session lasted for 25 minutes.

172-111713

WHITE BRIGHT LIGHT

My soul encountered white light frequently...

After meditation, I went back to bed lying on my left. Initially, I saw various images before any dreams. I saw a French door and I focused on it. Just like the zoom feature on a camera, the scene became larger, clearer and more focused. I felt myself being sucked into it.

I was no longer just watching the image but being in it. There was another door to the right of the French door. I directed my right hand out to turn the doorknob to open the door. Instantly, I was flying through a maze of indoor corridors and rooms.

When I reached a door, I opened it and there was nothing outside. However, I saw only white bright light illuminating the entire outer space. I did think of what my Teacher said in class. After sound and image, only light remains and nothing else. After that, I drifted into dreams for a short while before waking up. Session was only 10 minutes long.

MUSIC OF THE MANTRA

Mantra has its own workings, transcending all realms.

After 55' of meditation, I went back to bed lying on my left. My wife was also in bed. I actually lost my consciousness going into the transition state, not really knowing when it abruptly happened. As soon as I drifted into the transition state, I wanted to leave my body by rolling to my right. I did it for a few times but no follow through.

Instead, I started to roll to the left as if I would roll off the bed. It worked. Although there were distractions from my wife, I ignored them and continued floating out of the room into the living room.

I was directing both Dharma Seals at the wall to see if there were any changes. There was none. However, I heard the recitation of the 9words Mantra but not coming from me. It sounded like its musical version. I also tried to take a good look at my hands. I saw the actual hand sign with my right hand.

My wife was trying to hold me back and I ran out of the house through the front door anyway. Once I was outside, there appeared to be a multitude of fast evolving patterns of diamonds and crystals. They were well arranged images. I was elated seeing them.

Drifting into the next scene, I was in a large pool with icy crystals above me. There were openings but they were closing one by one as I approached them from below, until they were all closed.

Somehow, I got out through the top layer. I found myself in a large room. The scene became very colorful, vivid and real. I couldn't make out the things around me, but I was excited and anxious to check out everything closely.

Once I got out to the outside, there was open space and sky. I tried to fly away but felt being glued to the ground. I woke up thereafter. It was a 15-minute session.

174-121713
HUMAN ANATOMY

Human body has a nonphysical perspective.

After 45' of meditation, I went back to bed. Earlier before that, I had to get up to take medication for a stomachache. When I became awaken in my dreams, I effortlessly left my body. I didn't feel like I went anywhere. I was merely just a point in space seeing all kinds of things, such as clouds and smoke, rotating all around me. There were also inanimate images which I couldn't recognize or describe.

Suddenly, all my attention focused on the dead center of my field of vision. Something very small slowly became larger and larger, brighter and clearer.

At that moment, I thought that's probably how things originated from nothingness in space. It was absolute and nothing vague about it. That image changed into a sagittal cross section of a person's head and torso. There were 3 sacs of irregular border, like the linings of the intestines, expanding and contracting. They even moved slightly outside of the torso. Promptly, they changed into more than three. I was not surprised. I seem to be expecting and familiar with seeing organs of a human. I woke up thereafter. It was a 20-minute session.

175-012714
ENTITIES IN OTHER DIMENSIONS

Unpleasant looking beings exist in all realms.

After 55' of meditation, I went back to bed lying on my left. I nudged to the right and initiated the separation process. As I was leaving the body, I heard some unpleasant noise right next to me in bed.

After I detached completely from my body, I was facing a hazy fuzzy entity in front of me while I was standing. Immediately, I started to recite the 9words Mantra and directing my right Dharma Seal at it. However, it didn't go away fast enough so I even started to recite the Repentance Prayer.

From there, I drifted back to the transition state, but I wanted to continue. This second time around, I found myself in the open in a city facing a huge octopus looking robotic monster.

176-012814
HANGING UPSIDE DOWN

The superposition property of different realms.

After 60' of meditation, I went back to bed lying on my left. I stopped doing the nudging to the right. I would just think about leaving the body. Quickly, I was rolling to the right, feeling and seeing my arm and leg flinging over to the right.

This was the first time I stopped being totally passive. I started consciously to move my legs, to stand and to walk. Once I stood up, I wanted to be in charge, I hopped a little and floated out of the room supinely.

I saw my family in the study and living room. My legs felt light, and they kept floating up to the ceiling. The living room scene reminded me of the actual room before the remodeling. My wife was there, and I wanted to show her that I could stick my feet to the ceiling, upside down like a bat.

I went out to the balcony where I wanted to fly but didn't take up much height. I felt the houses outside seemed fake. Moving on to the next scene, I felt a little tired, thinking I just might be out too long. I saw a calendar, but I told myself that I won't find a date because there's no time. Nevertheless, I torn that page off, folded and put it in my back pocket. I would want to check it against my real world after I woke up.

I approached a lady whom I didn't know. I told her that I wanted to know her here even though we didn't know each other in my real world. She wanted something apparently from my real wife. I advised her against any black magic. I picked a spot to spin to wake up but to no effect. A moment later, the scene froze and faded. I woke up afterwards. It was a 25-minute session.

177-021014
PERCEPTION IS REALITY

---

*Belief is powerful...creating individual realities
in different realms.*

After 60' of meditation, I went back to bed lying on my left. I drifted into the transition state. By thinking of leaving the body, the process was completed.

However, right after crossing over the interface of the two realms, I felt out of breath due to holding. That caused me recoiled back into my body. But I knew I still have another chance. The second time around, I just let it happen without any of my will.

While I was going through the process the second time, I told myself that there's no actual breathing in or out, nor any holding or gasping of breath in the nonphysical side. Right away, my sensation of out of breath disappeared. Instantly, I was like a rocket going straight up, blasting off again and again but I still couldn't get out of the house.

Afterwards, I stopped inside of my room. I saw some colorful and clear images of stuff animals. I still just wanted to get out of the room. I squeezed myself slowly through the glass door to the outside. There was a large yard with trees.

I went over to touch the branches and felt the pricking of the needle leaves.

While I was reciting the 9words Mantra and holding my two Dharma Seals together, I asked to be taken to China. I showed up in a house of Chinese style. Their old-fashioned kitchen was down at the basement level. A young girl wanted to show me a hairy worm. During the whole time, I had this underlying mood that whatever I saw was meaningless. It was a 20-minute session.

178-021514
TELEPHOTO VISION

Soul's seeing is both microscopic and macroscopic.

After 60' of meditation, with a stuffy nose I went back to bed lying on my left side. At the time, birds outside were chirping. At the transition state, I was seeing vivid images limited to my forehead area. I couldn't recognize or remember any of the images.

This reminded me of my Teacher talking about seeing through the eyelids and emerging images. Then I called out my Teacher and He actually appeared momentarily.

Immediately after, I just felt a very quick detachment from my body. A short moment later, I was in a room drawing the curtains and looked out of the window. I knew if I saw something different, then I would be somewhere else.

I saw a great number of people crowded down on the streets. Apparently, I was ten floors up in a building. Those people were not very clear, and I knew if I chose to zoom in on any one of them, he would become clear.

Suddenly, I heard bees buzzing right in front of me on the window. I stood back and directed both of my Dharma Seals at those bee-like creatures.

Afterwards, I went to turn the doorknob, opened the door and went outside. I saw a woman in a chair by the desk. I called her to see if she was my wife. She showed her face that I didn't recognize. I woke up thereafter. Session was 20 minutes long.

179-030414
MY OTHER WIFE

The "Wan" symbol is one of the most important totems in Buddhism.

After 60' of meditation with straight back, feeling energized and I went back to bed lying on my left side. During the transition state, I was focusing on the images in front of me, rather than the out of body process. I also remembered my Teacher talking about emerging images.

At the same time, I noticed the familiar signals coming on. Before I could even realize any movements, I was already going through many rooms in a very large fancy and beautiful house. I noticed this was quite different from what I used to end up in, dark and unappealing. This house was vivid, bright and colorful.

Not long afterwards, I left that house and flying through space. There was this strong pressure against the bottom of my feet as I flew, giving me a sense of push-off power in flight and lightning speed.

While I was in space, I reached out to my right and felt a woman's forearm. I was surprised but not frightened. I held her arm and brought her around to face me. I was curious who could that be?

When she appeared, she was not my current wife. She also didn't look Chinese. We were both facing each other in space and with our own legs crossed. She was talking about our children, apparently, she was also my wife. We slowly descended back to the ground. We both were going through places with a lot of people.

Straightaway, I questioned her on what year it was and what country we were in. At first, she kept quiet. But moments later, she said something resembling a Chinese character "Wan" which meant ten thousand. I pondered over a thousand year which was too ancient. Or ten thousand years which would mean in the future.

After that realization, I waved goodbye to her and others. I said out loud, "I'm from your past and I'll see you in the future."

While I was walking around on the outside, suddenly, I felt like swimming through some shallow water. When I dived in, I didn't get too far. My right hand got poked by something sharp. I thought I would see a bloody wound when I woke up.

Next moment, I got up and took off flying. I asked to go to the moon. I should be able to see the "Jade Rabbit" over there. My two feet felt like two jet exhausts. The more pressure I felt, the faster I flew.

I felt energized and not anxious to wake up. Nevertheless, it all somehow stopped, and I woke up to a false awakening. I was at a dinner and people were serving a big block of Hong Kong style waffles. Slowly, I woke up from that. It was a 25-minute session.

180-032814
A TERRIFYING EXPERIENCE

An example of violent and scary encounter in another dimension.

I went to bed at 12:30 am. I slept for a while and woke up a little after 1:00. As I went back to sleep, I had this urge to go somewhere consciously. I knew I was already at the transition state. Quickly, I drifted into a lucid dream with myself still in bed, still lying on my left and eyes closed. I wanted to be more relaxed for the experience.

It started out with all sorts of movements of the bed, shaking, vibrating, up and down violently. All these caused corresponding feelings of sinking, pressing, pushing, squeezing and shaking upon me. Right away, I recited the 9words Mantra.

Without rest, it progressed into moving, pulling and ruffling of my blanket behind my back. Gradually, I was feeling something was right next to me. It evolved to a point that I was feeling hands lightly touching all over me, and elbow pressing down on my neck. This entity of some kind also pressed down on my entire body until finally, I felt it gave up. Instantly, something was lifted off from me. It was like it's waiting for me to respond.

Moment later, I was watching a movie about two large human creatures fighting. I felt it was behind me, also watching the movie. During the whole experience, I maintained my position, poise, mind set and the recitation of the 9words Mantra. I also stayed clear of fear, panic and emotions, even though at times I didn't know how far it would go on. But underneath all that, I knew I won't be harmed out of faith. All took only 10 minutes. I woke up and wrote this up immediately.

181-092914
MY GUIDING LIGHT

The afterlife does have a literally "Dark" side...

After 40'of meditation, I went back to bed lying on my left side. When I was aware of myself being in the transition state, just the thought of leaving the body would instantly complete the process.

Next moment, I ran out to the hallway with both of my arms out to the sides touching the wall and cabinets. They felt real. I quickly opened the front door and got out. During the whole time, it was dark and dim. I did notice a bright light balled up at the bottom of my visual field. It followed me like a shadow.

When I was outside, I was stunned to see nothing but pitch darkness without anything visible. I just took off flying superman style with no destination. From there, I woke up in the transition state. I didn't move or tried to get up. I ended up seeing that same white light still following me.

Note: I woke up feeling that there's nothing in my self nature. I started to get this new appreciation for the mundane world in front of me.

182-100214
THE ULTIMATE VOID

Only an absolute emptiness can serve as a platform for all possibilities.

After 90' of meditation, I went back to bed lying on my left. This time, I wasn't in a hurry and just flowed with it. The body detachment part was quick, and slowly I drifted out to the hallway. Since I didn't really know where to go, suddenly, I recoiled back into the body in the bedroom.

The second time around, it seemed a lot brighter. In the room, I slowly tried to go straight up to the ceiling and through the roof. Once I was out, I was surprised not seeing the expected open space, but instead a narrow, tall and straight wall enclosure.

I was struggling to climb up and eventually above the wall to the open. I looked around and I saw nothing but darkness. I broke down in tears, shouting, "Buddhas and Bodhisattvas let me know that there's nothing but emptiness."

Immediately, the scene changed, and dreams came in. There was a kid kept following me. He was looking for my younger son. I kept saying that I've been out for too long. I needed to go back. But they wanted me to help someone at the ER.

183-102714
BUDDHA ON THE WALL

Finally, a divine manifestation...

After 40' of meditation, I went back to bed lying on the left. I didn't pay much attention to the signal. Unexpectedly, the separation from my body had already occurred. I was drifting in the room with a clear scene. I had no purpose and didn't know what to do or where to go.

Suddenly, I remembered to recite the 9words Mantra and directing my two Dharma Seals at the wall. Image of the head of the Buddha appeared. Then I remembered my Teacher and His Teacher. After few more recitations, the image on the wall somehow changed a bit.

Then I opened the curtains and just wanted to go outside. Once I was out, it was bright and vivid. I flew straight up but stuck at a certain height. I looked down, seeing very unfamiliar objects doing their activities below in the city. It was a 20-minute session.

184-111014
HOLDING MY OWN HEAD

Message from the spiritual world can be direct and blunt.

After 60' of meditation, I went back to bed lying on my left. Without signals, the detachment process started with me facing down in my physical body. It went on for a while.

Just like that, I was standing with my left arm extended straight out holding my own head. I recognized it was me. Straightaway, the face started changing from one grotesque face to another continuously for a while. They were all unrecognizable deformed figures.

At first, I was a little startled, but I quickly calmed down. I was thinking the message could be that I'm not the face and yet I'm all the faces. I drifted into other dreams before I woke up.

185-121514
THE DORMANT SENTIMENT

Important sentimental events accumulate in our souls.

After 60' of meditation, I went back to bed lying on my left side. The transition state and the body detachment process both were skipped.

Out of nowhere, I just showed up in a dark room. I was sitting back and pointed my left finger out in the front. There was a bright white light at the fingertip. I made Dharma Seal with both hands and directed them forward. However, I saw my hands in wavy dark forms.

In a flash, I just took off through the roof to the outside. I flew around at low altitude. I could see clearly the city scene. Slowly, I lost the energy to stay up and landed.

I was going through the streets where people were fixing up the store front. There was a person in front calling me doctor. I looked at the white coat that I was apparently wearing. I caught a glimpse of the name tag which appeared to be the name of the place where I had worked for twenty years. The name was clear at first but just quickly faded away. Note: I was terminated just few weeks ago.

Right away, I was weeping tears feeling a sentiment which I couldn't understand. I was at one time this other person and the only thing that would remain after all was emotion. I woke up afterwards. Session was 30 minutes long.

186-010515
TAHITI REVISITED

Body and soul might have different experiences.

After 50' of meditation, I went back to bed lying on my left side. I drifted off to dreams at first but woke up at the transition state. I decided to place my focus at my upper right corner area. I felt something moving in my body but not enough to kick start the out of body process. So instead, I switched my focus on being out of my body completely and it just happened.

At the foot of the bed, I said to myself that I wanted to know my causality with my wife. Then I held my hands together and pointed straight up above my head, attempting to fly off. Instead, I hit something up in the ceiling. I didn't go anywhere.

I was at the glass door drawing the curtains and saw a brush hedge right outside. I also saw numerous plants all over the patio. Immediately, I knew it was not my real physical house. I walked out to the patio where I saw a steep slope, quite a long one, leading down to the sea.

There were houses at the foot of a pointed rising mountain peak. I knew it was Tahiti where my wife and I had our honeymoon. Then I flew off, gliding slowly across the sky to look at the dwellings on the left, the sea and the peak on my right. Soon after, I ended up at a place where I was talking to a woman. She said we had a history. It was a 45-minute session.

187-042815
EMPATHY OF THE ESSENCE

Rediscovering the compassion in my soul...

After 30' of meditation, I went back to bed lying on my left side. Unconsciously I drifted into dreams and awakened in the transition state. I remembered to nudge to the upper right direction. Quickly, I rolled out to the right, but it didn't last. So, I rolled back into my physical body. Without a pause, I kept rolling to the left until I left the body.

Thereafter, I didn't stay too long in the room. I showed up in open streets where there were a lot of people. I saw two large wheels with people on them. Then slowly, all of them disappeared from the scene. Simultaneously, I was reciting the 9words Mantra and directing both of my Dharma Seals outward bestowing blessings in all directions. I got quite sentimental at that moment.

Before long, people started showing up again and surrounded me, passing out to me their business cards. They were of different nationalities and very friendly. Gradually, it got blurry. I did ask for the year and tried to find it on a calendar. I offered to teach a woman how to fly but instead, she wanted to show me how to fly. On our way out to the open, I woke up. The session was 15 minutes long.

188-020316
SEAMLESS SHIFTING OF REALITIES

A happy and joyous soul...

It had been nine months since my last time being out of the body. After 60' of meditation this morning, I went back to bed lying on my back. But I wasn't feeling completely at ease. My wife was still in bed sleeping and breathing hard. I changed to my usual left sleeping position. I was thinking it was not going to happen.

Then I remembered to mentally nudge to the upper right direction and right away I felt something moving within me. Great, it was going to happen soon. But instead, I felt my wife turning over to my side and touching me.

Meanwhile, I needed to go to the bathroom. All my stuff were in the wrong place and her things were everywhere. She was right behind me. I was upset and questioned her. Right at that moment, I realized I was in a different world. I turned out to be very happy.

After we went back to bed, I saw three teenage boys, apparently my sons. Nevertheless, I didn't recognize them. Note: I have two adult sons in the physical world. I asked each one of them for their names. They all said Luke. One of them told me that people making fun of their names, Luke Luke Luke.

I was so happy and joyous walking out of the house, knowing that I was in another world. Then I saw my father, mother, brother and sister. The entire family I grew up with in the physical world. I didn't say who I was. I wanted to test them to see if they knew me. They came by to greet me but not as a family member. My mother gave me a kiss on my cheek. They were praising me for reciting sutra and something else that I couldn't remember or understand. After a short moment, everything faded out and I woke up. It was 37 minutes long.

189-021516
A MATTER OF VISUALIZATION

My soul could also be playful.

After 25' of meditation, I went back to bed lying flat on my back. Shortly after, I ran into the doctor whom I used to work with before he passed away few years back. It took a while for him to recognize me.

I was in my long lab coat, riding a bike on my way to work. But I got lost on the streets. When I reached a busy intersection, I saw a large building which I recognized from before.

In the next scene, I attempted to put my right palm through the solid wall. It didn't work at first. Slowly, the heel of my palm started to sink in. Immediately after, I felt the power.

Seeing many people walking down the wide boulevard, I started fanning my two hands side to side, focusing on all those people in front of me. I created strong wind blowing over them and kicking up dust everywhere. I also used my index finger directing at some people nearby.

After that, I saw an army of people or beings marching towards me, apparently challenging me. I started to command myself to grow gradually in size, to a gigantic being overshadowing them. I woke up thereafter. Session was 15 minutes long.

190-021916
BREATHING UNDER WATER

An impossible experience...

In the regular night dreams, I was floating in a vast and calm ocean. I even wanted to take a picture of it. Suddenly, a large wave rose up in front of me and came down over me. Up to the point when I realized that I was drowning, everything was just dream-like. But as soon as I was able to breathe through my nose under water, this discrepancy jump-started my awareness into high alert.

From that point on, I could remember much more. I was so amazed that I jumped back into the water just to test out my new ability. This second time around, I was much more aware of my breathing through my nostrils, more so on my left nostril. It felt just like regular normal breathing.

I was so elated that I wanted to to tell my family after they brought me out of the water. I was about to tell my girlfriend and my wife, both of whom I didn't recognize. However, I got interrupted and it didn't happen.

191-071816
THE VOICE TO REMEMBER

Someone I can count on in the afterlife.

After 120' of meditation, I went back to bed lying on my left side. This is my new residence. I quickly detached from my body and landed by the window. I didn't want to stay there too long. I drew the curtains seeing numerous high-rise apartments, all broken down and damaged. Then I moved around to other rooms. I heard clearly my Teacher's voice doing a lecture. As I approached, it was a recorder of some kind. I bowed and paid my respect. I couldn't remember much thereafter due to late recollection.

192-072516
MY THREEFOLD PERSPECTIVES

The amazing nature of my soul...

This was my first time to experience being out of body during meditation. At the time, I was staying in a temporary residence without my altar. This familiar subtle signal before the out of body process suddenly came on. I recognized it and I mentally gave my body a little nudge backward. It worked.

I levitated slowly upward out of my body. I remained sitting straight and crossing my legs, hovering about 3 feet off the floor. While I was levitating, I also had the vision of a dark image of myself hovering in front of me. I was quite indifferent about it without any reaction.

I did however want to fly away somewhere else. But I gradually felt out of breath in my real physical body, and I just dropped back into my body. Only then, I realized my upper body was curving forward without a straight back.

After 120' of meditation, I went back to bed lying on my left side. I drifted into a dreamy transition state. I felt vividly I was out of my body and moving to another scene.

I was under a train like vehicle and above the track. I said to myself that I shouldn't be here for too long. Moment later, I realized it was a roller coaster. I was riding with it in excitement through the entire track. It felt very real. After I got off the roller coaster, I met up with my two sons in their early teens. I went through a false awakening before waking up. This long session lasted for 60 minutes.

193-081116
WE'RE THE WORLDS

My soul knows more than my physical mind.

After 120' of meditation, I went back to bed lying on my back. Again, it was very hard to know when I drifted into the transition state. That subtle indescribable signal came. I nudged backward and the same signal came again. At the third time, I got out of my body.

I felt like being in an energy vortex, taking on tremendous number of intense vibrations and shaking. At one point, I was a little concerned, thinking it might be something bad. Immediately, I recited the 9words Mantra.

Shortly after, I ended up very close to a wall full of unfamiliar totems akin to my Teacher's drawings. I was trying to take it all in. A while later, the wall started showing world maps with different countries' names. I remembered China but I couldn't make much out of the rest. The last map shown was the old map of Atlantis.

As I drifted away from the wall, I became active and not being passive. There was nothing remarkable afterwards, except me jumping down stories of a building. The session was 30 minutes long.

194-071918
REALITIES OF VISUALIZATION

My soul can be seen as a portal to other realms.

After 120' of meditation, I went back to bed lying flat on my back. At the right upper area, I started to visualize a nice scene with two opposing cliffs at the seashore. The entire image became larger and larger while I was still aware of being in bed trying to sleep.

As I was drifting more into the image, it became more vivid and lively and simultaneously I gradually lost my awareness of being in bed. By the time I merged totally with the image, I saw a lot of otherworldly images flying around that were beyond me. The last scene was me flying into space marveling the constellations in space. I went through a false awakening before waking up.

195-072418
MY INNER TEMPLE

Establishing my own sacred land...

After only 60' of meditation due to pain in my right knee, I went back to bed lying on my back. Just out of the blue, I found myself levitating upright and floating through an assembly with a lot of people, apparently familiar to me. I did hesitate to float in front of them for not wanting them to perceive it as a showoff.

As I floated out of the two huge halls, I bowed to the towering Buddha Statue. I also passed by many students attending my Teacher's class. I floated down the staircase and even over a wall. In the end, I lost heights and about to touch the ground. I woke up thereafter. It was a 30-minute session.

196-081118
PORTAL IN MY MIND

My soul practically just leaped into another dimension...

After two hours of meditation, I went back to bed lying on my back. I started seeing unfamiliar images appearing while I was still aware of being in bed. During this transition state, I began to focus more on the image.

While I was following the image, I visualized myself merging with it. As soon as I started doing that, that familiar and subtle shock signal came upon me. This phenomenon pushed me over completely into the scene of the image, thereby, losing my awareness of being in bed.

Shortly after, I was floating like fish in water, from room to room. When I reached a small tight dead end, I looked up and found a round opening to the sky. I gazed at the opening and the scene froze up. Right away I knew I was about to wake up.

Nevertheless, I said to myself to just take me. Immediately after, the scene started to move again and resumed. I did it one more time taking charge of the fading image, so that the scene could prolong. Session was about an hour long.

197-082718
DEEP INTO THE MAZE

A deep realization that my soul is always watching over me.

In the early morning of 3:00, I woke up and couldn't go back to sleep. So, I meditated for 45' and still couldn't go back to sleep. My mind was full of thoughts on on the writing of my realizations and insights.

After another full hour of meditation, I went back to bed at 5:30. My wife came into the bathroom making a lot of noise. While I was on the verge of falling asleep, every sound she made was like a shock wave through my being.

Finally, she left and immediately I shifted into the transition state. I was conscious and gave a nudge to my upper right direction. I floated right out of my body.

For a moment, I couldn't decide to float, glide horizontally or just fly away. I stood up without touching the floor and glided out of the room. While I was flying up in the open, I felt tight pressure under both of my armpits. As if someone was holding me up. When I landed, I recited the 9words Mantra and the pressure was gone.

Before long, I found myself vividly back in bed, but it was only a false awakening. Again, I glided out of the room. While

I was looking around, my older son in his preteen walked in towards me.

He had pimples on his face, and we hugged. I was thinking just how nice it must be for people to do this to meet their loved ones. I was moved and started crying. Nevertheless, I also knew full well that my crying in this scene was completely separated from my actual physical life.

Once again, I was back going through another false awakening in my bathroom. I realized the deeper I went, the more detached I was from the awareness of my actual real world. I started to get a little confused. I was concerned about being out too long and still not waking up.

At that moment, my younger son joined in, and I hugged both. I even said, "Aren't you guys supposed to be 30 years old?" They both looked like ten years old. We all went outside and saw a line of giant Pokémon characters.

I also asked them what I do for a living. When I told them I must go back now, my older son dug up a package with the name of an Olympic athlete and his wife's picture on it. I did not recognize either one of them, but I had this feeling that I was supposed to contact her.

This time, I woke up still to another scene, but I held still until I finally woke up. My physical body was solidly frozen. I couldn't move anything but my dry mouth. I slowly turned my head to see the clock. I was gone for 40 minutes. It took a while for me to get back into all parts of my body. I was attempting to get up to write but I got dizzy and went back to sleep.

198-030423
LEAPING BETWEEN REALMS

My soul knew how to defend against hostility.

After 25' of early morning meditation, I went back to bed lying on my left. I was thinking that I might not be able to fall asleep, due to some disturbing news.

There were still images appearing in my mind. I started to command myself to leap into it. With the first few attempts, I was getting that familiar signal of vibration. It was getting stronger as I kept attempting to jump in. In the last attempt, I sensed that, "I got in" and "Breaking out of my body".

I was upright and moving up higher, swirling around the dark room at the same time. I ended up high in a room which I didn't recognize. I knew I was in another place. I wanted to make sure that I didn't forget to recite the 9words Mantra, which I did. And I felt good about doing that.

I thought I was about to wake up. I did try to think of the universe, so that I could fly there but to no avail. I was just feeling slowly waking up in bed. At that moment, I heard a man talking to me. Gradually, he appeared and held on my hands tightly. I found that unpleasant and hostile. Immediately, I recited the 9words Mantra continuously, directing at him. That really pushed him and he slowly dropped down to the side of of my bed. While he was down, I directed my left Dharma Seal at him.

Suddenly, everything became very vivid in the room. I moved from room to room, seeing green bamboos on the side of the hallway. My son was with me. We attempted to go outside, but it was too bright, and we came back in.

Eventually, we ended up in a restaurant setting. When I asked others about what city and state, they stayed quiet and gradually all walked away. Then we walked to another place. I was thinking that I should be going back, being out too long.

My legs were feeling weak. I was thinking that it must be due to sleeping on the side, one leg pressing on the other. Then I was at a marketplace where I saw my childhood friend. I even asked my wife to meet her. Slowly I woke up. The session was 40' long. I was feeling very energetic and not tired at all afterwards.

199-060823
INFINITE DOUBLE DOORS

My soul was full of sentiments.

After 30' of meditation, I went back to sleep. I experienced a quick crossover before settling on the floor. Immediately I had sprung into action and roaming around the house, checking here and there. There was nothing special and kind of boring.

I flew up into the sky for a while. Everything seemed unreal and looked fabricated. One thing that I could remember was opening a double door closet but kept seeing the same closed double doors. I did it multiple times with the same image of only the double doors.

I did feel strange. The feeling that I had was emptiness, meaninglessness, unreal, dim, boring and lifelessness. I didn't know how long it lasted. While I was roaming around, I felt the need to go back. When the image froze up, I knew I was heading back. I even intentionally focused on how the image fading away.

Note: I asked for some money, and it appeared in a stack of bills

200-071523
WATCHING AND FEELING

My soul could be at two places at the same time.

After 30' of meditation, I went back to bed lying on my left side. In the state of transition, I felt the onset of the subtle signals. They were familiar but indescribable.

All sudden, I was able to simultaneously see and feel my curled body rising up from the bed. Once I settled down to the floor, I was anxious to leave the dim room. I remembered that I recited the 9words Mantra.

I tried to fly through the ceiling with my hands together pointing up, but to no avail. Thus, I gave up and resorted to opening door to other parts of the house. I saw a woman in a room with opening to the outside. I asked for clarity, and it became bright and clear.

Before I flew out to the outside, I turned her around to see if she was my wife. Although her image wasn't clear, I knew she was. I was only able to hover over tall apartment buildings below me. The session was 30' long and I wasn't aware when I came back.

CONCLUSION

If you have traveled as me through these 200 journeys, you probably would develop some very different definitions on the concept of a soul than before. Just the idea of an entity deeply embedded inside of a person is mind-boggling. However, as long as we can stay true to the objectivity of the events, the fundamental nature of human existence will reveal itself.

You probably wonder how this book would help with the problems in our mundane lives. An over-thinking mind and unstable state of emotion, contribute to most of our problems. Here and now, you know you can never be alone in confronting life, and that's comforting. Your soul in its subtle way, will always be your guiding light.

Made in United States
Troutdale, OR
12/09/2024